For
Frits Markus

VALUE JUDGEMENT

Improving our Ethical Beliefs

JAMES GRIFFIN

CLARENDON PRESS · OXFORD

Oxford University Press, Great Clarendon Street, Oxford OX2 6DP

Oxford New York

Athens Auckland Bangkok Bogota Bombay
Buenos Aires Calcutta Cape Town Dar es Salaam
Delhi Florence Hong Kong Istanbul Karachi
Kuala Lumpur Madras Madrid Melbourne
Mexico City Nairobi Paris Singapore
Taipei Tokyo Toronto Warsaw

and associated companies in
Berlin Ibadan

Oxford is a trade mark of Oxford University Press

Published in the United States by
Oxford University Press Inc., New York

First published 1996
First issued in paperback 1997

British Library Cataloguing in Publication Data
Data available

Library of Congress Cataloging in Publication Data
Griffin, James, 1933-
Value Judgement / James Griffin.
Includes bibliographical references and index.
1. Values. I. Title.
BD232.G667 1996 170'.42—dc20 96-10751
ISBN 0-19-823553-4
ISBN 0-19-875231-8 (Pbk)

Printed in Great Britain
on acid-free paper by
Bookcraft (Bath) Ltd
Midsomer Norton, Avon

VALUE JUDGEMENT

PREFACE

The material in this book had its first outing in 1989 when I was invited to be a Visiting Professor by the Greater Philadelphia Philosophy Consortium. I particularly remember helpful criticism of my lectures there from Jay Wallace, Michael Krausz, Gerald Vision, and Andrew Levine.

I had started writing the lectures with a few rough but firm ideas that I wanted to develop and test. One was that much philosophical discussion of cognitivism, objectivism, and realism in ethics was conducted at too abstract a level, and too abstract in different ways. First, it tried to reach strong conclusions about ethics from quite general considerations about meaning and knowledge, whereas I thought, to the contrary, that merely identifying models of cognitivism, objectivity, and realism that ethics might find easier to comply with fell well short of showing that it actually did comply with them. One needed, I thought, to pay much more attention to how we actually arrived—and, more importantly, had to arrive —at our ethical decisions. I could not see how we could reach interesting conclusions in metaethics without reaching some fairly hefty ones in normative ethics. And, second, much current philosophical discussion treated values and value judgements as homogeneous, whereas I thought that they were strikingly heterogeneous and that little of interest could be said about them in general. I also started off a bit sceptical of talk about the 'justification' of ethics, of ethical 'theories', even of 'method' in ethics (cp., of course, justification and theories and method in science). And I was more than a little sceptical about the 'method', coherentism, that is nowadays almost universally accepted by philosophers. Coherentism did not seem to me necessarily wrong; it seemed to me to say so very little.

After a period without much focus for my various interests, I grouped them around the 'methodological' question, How, and how much, can we hope to refine our ethical standards? And that includes, but is hardly exhausted by, the question, How are we to decide the relative merits of the competing normative traditions—

utilitarianism, deontology, virtue ethics, and so on—that our culture takes most seriously? So my central question involved a step back from the debates between these competing traditions and asked what the terms of the debate are. But my doubts about the independence of normative ethics and metaethics made me sceptical about the possibility of stepping back—that is, stepping back from one lot of questions in ethics to another without carrying most of the first lot along with one. I found that answering my central question involved venturing an answer to most questions in ethics. And so my subject grew to its present, far from tidy shape.

The natural arc of my thought, I have discovered, is a book. Many of the articles that I have published in recent years have been early attempts at the chapters that follow. Chapter I is a much revised version of 'How We Do Ethics Now' from *Modern Ethics*, edited by A. P. Griffiths (Cambridge: Cambridge University Press, 1993). Parts of Chapter II first appeared in 'Against the Taste Model', in *Interpersonal Comparisons of Well-Being*, edited by J. Elster and J. Roemer (Cambridge: Cambridge University Press, 1991). Chapter III is a revision of 'Values: Reduction, Supervenience, and Explanation by Ascent', in *Reduction, Explanation, and Realism*, edited by D. Charles and K. Lennon (Oxford: Clarendon Press, 1992). Chapter VI contains material from 'On the Winding Road from Good to Right', published in *Values, Welfare and Morality*, edited by R. Frey and C. Morris (Cambridge: Cambridge University Press, 1993). Much of Chapter VII was first delivered as one of the William Galbraith Miller Lectures in Jurisprudence at the University of Glasgow, and will soon be published with the other lectures. I am grateful for permission to use this material here.

Again and again, I have been helped by criticism and, rarer but no less important, support from audiences at lectures, seminars, and conferences. That my bad memory prevents me from mentioning everyone who helped is no reason not to thank the few whom I do recall, who are Michael Smith, Ezra Heymann, Peter Sandøe, Klemens Kappel, Rodolfo Vázquez, John Dunn, Mark Platts, Margarita Valdés, Robert Stern, and Christopher Hookway. I now wish I had recorded my debts as I incurred them.

Joseph Raz and I gave a class together just when I started collecting my thoughts on the subjects in this book, and I benefited greatly from it. Ruth Chang, Roger Crisp, Esperanza Guisán, Brad

Hooker, Javier Rodríguez Alcázar, and John Tasioulas read all, or most, of an earlier draft. And I could not have hit it luckier than I did with the anonymous referees chosen by the Press. These are the people to whom my debt is greatest.

J. P. G.

Keble College
Oxford

CONTENTS

INTRODUCTION

We inherit our ethical standards. We start our moral life with firm views about right and wrong, some so firm that they are never shaken. Still, in time we start rejecting others of them. We do not just change our minds about them; we also find them faulty in some way—unjustified, out of date, too undiscriminating. We regard our new ethical beliefs as not just different, but better.

Much moral philosophy should be seen as just a continuation—more self-conscious and more sustained—of this project of improvement that all of us are engaged in well before we have even heard of philosophy. Some philosophers think they find a single foundational ethical principle, or a fairly small set of principles, by appeal to which we can sort our inherited standards into sound and unsound, and so rebuild our originally rather ramshackle ethical beliefs into a firmer structure. Other philosophers think they find a particularly fundamental, authoritative way to deliberate about ethical questions that will lead to more reliable answers. Those are ambitious projects, and it is by no means certain that they have succeeded.

This book answers the question, How, and how much, can we hope to improve our ethical standards? It is not the largely psychological question of how we are to raise our standards of behaviour—that is, lift our behaviour closer to our standards—but how we are to refine the standards themselves. That, surely, is a philosophical question, but it is at several removes from a lot of the debate in moral philosophy. Much of that debate is devoted to developing a substantive ethical position—for example, utilitarianism or Kantianism or virtue ethics—and arguing for it over the others. My question is at some remove, because it asks, How should we choose between these competing positions? It is perhaps at some further remove still, because it does not assume that we have to choose any of them. The major substantive ethical positions, the ones that have for the most part dominated the history of philosophy, for all their differences, have one thing in common: they are highly ambitious; they believe that the critical standards that philosophy brings to bear on our inherited views are quite considerable. I start with a question that does not make that assumption. How great are our critical powers?

It is better at the start not to think of this, as in philosophy we sometimes do, as the question of 'method' in ethics. The word 'method' suggests a universal critical procedure, and there may be only various piecemeal forms of criticism. It also tends to suggest the two 'methods' that dominate discussion of how one 'justifies' a body of thought: foundationalism and coherentism. That one or the other of them suits ethical beliefs is far too strong an assumption to begin with.

My wish in this book is to start where anyone would be willing to start. Of course, I should like then to take them with me all the way to my destination. As that is impossible, there is a certain perverse folly in even trying. I should have to try to design arguments that would drag everyone, whatever the intellectual source of their resistance, along with me. It would not work. My subject does not lend itself to that kind of rigour. One might succeed in making every argument that one actually deployed watertight. But one does not usually go seriously wrong in philosophy over details of one's argument. One goes seriously wrong in the biggest things, in the things one does not even think of, in one's whole orientation. At the very best, one's orientation will allow one a glimpse of an important truth or two, but it will also certainly be responsible for one's overlooking a dozen others. In philosophy generally, and certainly in the sort of project I am embarking on, we are at present, and always shall be, groping in the dark simply to get a sense of some of the large contours of our subject. One's only reasonable hope is that, by groping, one will find something, and that others will take a look.

I

IMPROVING OUR ETHICAL BELIEFS

1. *Piecemeal appeal to intuition*

Our ethical standards are hand-me-downs, and sooner or later we start criticizing them. How should we go about it?

Among philosophers, the most common sort of criticism nowadays is what can be called piecemeal appeal to intuition. We are all familiar with how it goes. 'It follows from your view that it would be all right to do such-and-such. But that's counter-intuitive. So your view must be wrong.' Philosophers do not use the word 'intuition' here, as in earlier times, to refer to a special way of knowing; instead, they mean by it merely a moral sentiment or belief that persons have independently of any moral theory or philosophy that they might adopt.

Philosophers now pretty much agree that, as criticism, piecemeal appeal to intuition is weak, though, for lack of anything stronger, their belief has not had the revolutionary effect on their practice that one might reasonably expect to follow.

It is not that piecemeal appeal to intuition shows nothing. It is just that the doubts that it raises are very strong.[1] It may well be that some intuitions are as sound moral beliefs as we shall ever get. Others, however, clearly are not, and there are no internal marks distinguishing the first lot from the second. Intuitions, despite the misleading suggestion in their name of a special sort of perception into moral reality, are just beliefs. Some of those beliefs have been drummed into us in our youth by figures of authority, and are no more reliable than those figures were. Some are social taboos that, if we understood their origin, we would see are now obsolete. Some are edicts of the perhaps unfortunate super-ego that emerged from our private battle with our own aggression. And so on. What slight knowledge we have of the origins of our moral beliefs hardly leads us to grant them, as a kind, a lot of authority.[2] Causal explanations are not equally corrosive, of course. Some leave us hesitant when before we were confident; some make us drop what before we held; some actually strengthen our beliefs. For the most part, though, we do not know the causes of our intuitions. Even perfectly natural, nearly universally distributed sentiments and attitudes may not be in order as they are. For instance, it is natural—indeed, characteristic of human nature generally—for our sympathies to be warmly engaged by nameable persons whose lives are at risk but not by merely statistical lives; but it is not at all clear that governments are right to spend, as they usually do, far more on saving one missing yachtsman than it would take to save dozens of unknown lives through wider detection of cancer. And moral sentiments, attitudes, and beliefs are, like certain observations of supposedly brute facts, theory-laden, probably much more laden with theory than such observations are, and the theory can be poor. For instance, much of our moral vocabulary in English has a certain—to my mind, wrong-headed—model of moral relations built into it etymologically: the terms 'ought', 'should', 'duty', 'obligation', 'retribution', 'merit', 'rights', 'contract', all come originally from commerce or commercially oriented law, and have to do with owing, paying, binding, and so on.[3] It is natural for us to reach for relations that we understand to explain those that we do not, but there is no guarantee that our ancestors have always reached in the right direction. True, etymology is not meaning, but etymology can—and in this case does—shape our thinking in deep ways of which we are often unaware. It is no panacea even to take the most optimistic view about the soundness of some of our intuitions. Even if some are indeed perceptions of moral reality, we have also to wonder whether they are more than the merest glimpse of a fragment of reality, and whether, therefore, when reality's whole contour is eventually revealed, we might not view the fragment quite differently.

That, in very summary form, is the powerful negative case. It prompts the question, Should not the role that intuitions play in moral philosophy be no more nor less than the role that we are content to let them play in other branches of thought, in mathematics, in the natural sciences, and in other parts of philosophy? For instance, Russell's Theory of Types has strikingly counter-intuitive consequences for Boolean class algebra and the definition of numbers. Since the theory restricts a class to members of only one type, it has the result that Boolean algebra can no longer be applied across classes, but has to be reproduced within each type, and furthermore that numbers, defined on the basis of certain logical concepts, have similarly to be reduplicated for each type—consequences that W. V. Quine once condemned as 'intuitively repugnant'.[4] But no logician takes such repugnance as closing an argument. On the contrary, intuitive repugnance is just a spur to start looking for a good argument. Even if the role that intuitions should play in ethics is not entirely the same as in other branches of thought—I shall come to that matter in a moment—what I have called the negative case at least reinforces the view that piecemeal appeal to intuition is weak argument. It gives intuitions more weight than they deserve. It is especially in ethics that intuitions have risen so far above their epistemological station. That may be for the reason I mentioned earlier: where on earth are better arguments going to come from?

2. *Purist views*

A bold response to the inadequacy of piecemeal appeal to intuition is to become teetotal: to forswear all dependence on substantive moral beliefs, and to try instead to derive such beliefs from considerations that are themselves untainted by moral element. But is that possible?

Kant is the most famous purist—at least on a common, but disputed, reading of him.[5] On that reading, his aim is to derive substantive moral conclusions from formal features of rationality. What philosophers have in mind in speaking of reason and rationality varies greatly, from thin, irresistible, logical standards at one end to thick, contentious moral standards at the other. Kant looks like a purist because, at first glance, he seems to use the thinnest of conceptions, indeed only the notion of contradiction. His categorical imperative test involves, first, universalizing one's proposed maxim of action, adding this new law of human operation to a description of how the rest of the world operates, and then seeing whether contradiction results. But in some cases of even blatantly immoral maxims, it is very hard to uncover anything remotely approaching contradiction in the strict sense. But Kant explains that he has in mind either of two sorts of contradiction:

contradiction in formulation and contradiction in the will. And his explanation of, in particular, contradiction in the will draws upon a somewhat richer account of rationality. There is nothing wrong with this. But both this richer account of rationality and his use of a richer notion of contradiction as a test of right and wrong carry a certain freight of teleological views about human nature and, in the end, also moral views. A rich theory of rationality and a substantive moral theory can come hand in hand. When accounts of rationality get rich in this way, they get contentious. People differ about what count as moral reasons. How do we decide who is right? The decision, in the end, will not be merely about rationality unmixed with moral matters; it will be a choice of a substantive moral position. A widespread view—one that seems to me right—is that if Kant is read as appealing only to a thin enough conception of rationality to count as a purist, he does not succeed in deriving substantive moral conclusions; and that if he is read as enriching his conception of rationality enough for it to yield some substantive moral conclusions, then he is not a purist. Either way, we cannot point to Kant to show that purism is a live option.

There are modern purists, R. M. Hare[6] and R. B. Brandt[7] being prominent among them, but, to my mind, their forms of purism are too ambitious. I doubt that one can derive substantive moral principles from the logic of key moral terms (Hare) without the help of *some* substantive ethical beliefs. I doubt too that one can choose a reforming definition of ethics that will reduce it to a manageable factual project (Brandt) without *some* substantive ethical beliefs guiding the choice. I cannot myself see any form of purism that works.

3. *Have we been too hard on intuitions?*

Intuitions may not have great authority in ethics. But that is not to go so far as to say that they have no more authority than they do in mathematics or the natural sciences. That is because part of what ethics seeks to give expression to may be our self-understanding, our characteristic human sense of what matters. In ethics we ourselves, as we characteristically are, may be one of the central subjects of attention. This suspicion would be reinforced if it turned out, as I think it does,[8] that both reason and characteristic human desire have an important role in giving content to values. This point is related to a point about the human sciences: in the human sciences we are not only interpreting the world, but interpreting that part of it that includes centrally our interpretations of the world.[9] Ethical standards aim partly at giving expression to our sense of what matters, so one would expect the content of ethics to be already embedded in our intuitions—not necessarily in all of them but in some, not necessarily in undistorted form but in some form or other. One would expect ethical standards to display closer connections to our ordinary ethical thought, to our intuitions, than scientific laws need have to our intuitions about the natural world.

Perhaps, therefore, intuitions should be seen as common-sense beliefs. Some of them will no doubt be faulty, but there may be a core of them that form the unavoidable framework for all our thought. After all, there have been defences of common sense in the case of beliefs about the external world. Why not a similar defence of common sense in ethics? True, we have the large problem of how to distinguish unsound common-sense beliefs from sound ones; they can look exactly the same from the inside. But that some common-sense beliefs are duds should not, by itself, undermine our confidence in the whole lot. We do not conclude, just because our sense reports or our memory claims may occasionally be defective, that we must doubt them all. Instead, we trust the body of them—indeed, use them to pick out the duds among them. If we did not, we should lose the framework within which our concepts must operate.

Now, a similar argument is worth considering about morality. A word has meaning only in virtue of there being rules for its use, rules that settle whether the word is correctly or incorrectly used. And Wittgenstein argues that the rules cannot, in the end, be satisfactorily understood as a mental standard—an image, say, or an articulable formula—but only as part of shared practices. And these shared practices are possible only because of the human beliefs, interests, dispositions, sense of importance, and so on that go to make up what Wittgenstein calls a 'form of life'.[10] Our form of life provides the setting in which our language develops and only within which it is intelligibile. And a form of life seems to consist in part in a certain shared set of values. Donald Davidson has a similar argument. We cannot, he thinks, interpret the language that others use without assuming that we have certain basic beliefs and attitudes in common with them—that, for instance, many of our aims, interests, desires, and concerns are the same.[11] If that is right, then general scepticism about common-sense values is self-defeating. The values are embodied in the language we use, which sets for us the bounds of intelligibility.

There is force to these arguments of Wittgenstein and Davidson; the difficulty is to say how far they take us. How many such basic beliefs are there? How much can we mine from them? I shall come back to this later. To the extent that the criticism of ethics depends on such basic beliefs, the fewer there are, the slighter our critical powers are likely to be. Still, some of our 'intuitions' are such basic beliefs.

4. *The Coherence Theory*

Even so, the negative case against intuitions as a class still stands. So if we are to use intuitions to criticize our ethical beliefs, we shall have an altogether more powerful form of criticism if we can find a way of using intuitions critically, if we can sort the better from the worse. Some people think that we do that by making our beliefs coherent.

In the natural sciences we cannot test a hypothesis by seeing whether it squares with pure observation. Observation is not pure in the sense needed; our observations are themselves theory-laden. In the case of a conflict between a hypothesis and a report of an observation, therefore, sometimes the one and sometimes the other should give way. We have to be prepared to adjust each, going back and forth from theory to report, until the set of our beliefs reaches some sort of equilibrium. This procedure is not confined to the natural sciences; it also plays an important part in mathematics and logic. Axiomatic systems face the problem of showing that the axioms themselves are sound. If there can be no doubt about them—if they are, say, self-evident—then one has got a genuinely foundational form of justification: one can justify certain beliefs by deducing them from sound fundamental beliefs. But in much logic and mathematics, the starting-points are not beyond doubt. As the system of belief develops, pressures can build up to amend the starting-point rather than give up too much of the body of our beliefs. One might even find, in developing theories of meaning and truth, pressures building up to abandon, say, the law of excluded middle.[12] This sort of holism has claims to be the deepest form of rational procedure in all areas of thought.

The best procedure for ethics, it is plausible to think, is a similar one of going back and forth between intuitions about fairly specific situations on the one side and the fairly general principles that we use to try to make sense of our moral practice on the other, adjusting both, until eventually we bring them all into coherence. This is, I think, the prevailing view nowadays about how to improve our ethical beliefs.[13] It would indeed be likely to improve them. But how much?

This brings us on to the well-trodden ground of coherence theories. The coherence theory of truth (a theory about what truth consists in) raises many of the same issues as the coherence theory of justification (a theory about in what circumstances and to what extent a belief is credible), but it is the second that concerns us here. The coherence theory of justification holds that, ultimately, a belief is justified by, and only by, its being a member of a coherent set of beliefs.

The plausibility of that proposal rests crucially on how demanding 'coherence' is taken to be. Nowadays 'coherence' is thought of along these lines. 'Coherence' cannot demand only consistency; consistency constitutes a quite weak test for a set of beliefs. A conjunction of merely consistent beliefs is no more credible than its least credible member; if a belief of 20 per cent credibility is conjoined to a belief of 70 per cent credibility, the credibility of the conjunction is 20 per cent. The idea of 'coherence' has to capture how beliefs can support one another, how in aggregate they can pull up the reliability level of the set of beliefs as a whole. Perhaps consistency is not even a necessary condition of justification.[14] Many people's beliefs contain an inconsistency here or there in the whole set without much damaging the set's credibility. It is possible for one person's set of beliefs, though containing an inconsistency, to be much more justified on the whole than another person's set, though free of inconsistency.

Coherence cannot be a matter simply of consistency on a *wide* front, either. Adding the requirement that the set of beliefs be

comprehensive makes consistency more testing, but the test is still
fairly weak. It does not yet capture the bootstrap effect just mentioned. Nor does it meet the regress objection. The regress objection is that the credibility of one belief cannot depend upon that
of another without end; credibility must come from somewhere.
And merely to say that it comes from a set of beliefs as a whole
does not meet the objection. If one belief gets its credibility from
a second, and the second from a third, and so on until eventually,
circling back to the starting-point, some belief far on in the chain
of credibility transfers gets its credibility from the first, then we
have no explanation of how there is any credibility to be transferred in the first place. The way to meet the regress objection is
to reject the foundationalist presupposition at its heart, despite
the coherentist language it is sometimes expressed in. Justification, one should insist, is not linear—neither a straight line from
a starting-point, as foundationalists say, nor a circular line, as
coherentists might wrongly be thought to be saying. Coherentists
can maintain that some sets of beliefs are not just consistent con-
junctions but mutually supporting systems of belief, and that it is
their systematic connections that make them capable of raising
the credibility level of the whole set.

So we should take 'coherence' to mean an organization of beliefs
in a network of inferential relations. The most justificatorily powerful of such relations are explanatory ones, and the most powerful
example of organization that we have found so far is the sort of
'systematic unification', as Carl Hempel put it, provided by a natural
science.[15] Some contemporary supporters of the coherence theory
take such 'systematic unification' to be little different from the
concept of 'coherence'.[16] On that interpretation it is clear how
coherence can constitute a test of considerable power. To make
beliefs coherent is, in a way familiar from the natural sciences, to
verify or falsify them. It is also to test the adequacy of our conceptual framework; in developing an explanatory system, language
itself has often to change.[17]

Still, even on this rich interpretation of 'coherence', the coherence theory has problems. For one thing, there are many different coherent sets of beliefs incompatible among themselves. How
can a coherence theory single out one uniquely justified set?[18] For
another, a belief is justified, according to the coherence theory, by
its relations to other beliefs, not by its relation to the world. Can

a coherence theory find a place for perceptual input from a non-conceptual world? It must; for the aim of our empirical beliefs is to describe that world.

These two objections are closely linked. There are many—probably infinitely many—possible worlds different from the actual world yet describable equally coherently.[19] We distinguish between the actual and only possible worlds by perception, by input from a reality independent of our thoughts. Our beliefs about the world must be empirically grounded, and this grounding will lead us to a unique, most justified set.[20]

We believe, on the one hand, that the world around us impinges upon us, causes us to have the perceptions we have. We receive, we register, this independent world. These perceptual beliefs, therefore, have a high credibility, a credibility that arises from the closeness of their causal connection to this independent world. Yet, on the other hand, we also accept that no perceptual belief merely registers a thought-independent reality. We may to some degree be passive in perception, but we are also partly active: we interpret; we categorize. We have no access to a world behind our experience, entirely innocent of our interpretation, our language. And the justification of a perceptual belief cannot be independent of other beliefs—independent, in particular, of the general principle that the beliefs of direct awareness that arise in certain privileged circumstances are highly credible. What is more, any one perceptual belief is defeasible; whether we stand by it depends upon what turns up later.

So, a good coherence theory—indeed, any good theory of justification at all—must accommodate both direct awareness and the dependence of perceptual beliefs upon other beliefs. What is not easy to decide is whether the theory that manages this can still be a coherence theory,[21] or whether it must become a hybrid coherence-foundationalist theory,[22] or, indeed, whether the question is really now one for linguistic legislation. At the very least, the necessary accommodation of empirical input requires the abandonment of a certain simple form of coherentism—the form that holds, as coherentism in many of its formulations implies, that no one belief starts with greater credibility than any other, that there are no favoured beliefs with an initial credibility independent of coherence with the rest. Such an accommodation brings with it the abandonment of this pure democracy of beliefs. It may

take a large theoretical system to sanction the special authority of
perceptual beliefs, but what it sanctions is precisely that those
beliefs have a special authority because of how they relate to the
world, not simply because of how they relate to other beliefs.

It is hard, though, to gauge the consequences of that admis-
sion. It moves us to a theory that in some form or other allows
non-belief input (so may not be coherentist) but does not treat
perceptual beliefs as the starting-points of a one-way route of transfers of credibility (so does not seem to be foundationalist). What
is impossible to resist is not coherentism but holism. Holism is the
thesis that justification comes only from a whole set of beliefs.
Coherentism is just one version of that view: it gives a certain specification of what it is about the set that produces justification:
namely, that the beliefs form a system of inferential relations.
There is more logical space within holism than coherentism occu-
pies. Both foundationalism and coherentism offer pictures of the
overarching structure of credibility transfers. Simple foundationalism has starting-points—basic beliefs—of high credibility with
one-directional flows of credibility from them. Simple coherentism
has beliefs conferring credibility on other beliefs solely through
their own relations. The truth is bound to be more complicated
than either of these simple pictures captures. What exactly it is I
am going to leave aside. My interest is in our ethical beliefs, and
the pressing questions about them are quite different.

5. *A coherence theory for ethics*

The defence of the coherence theory that I have just sketched
depends upon its being a theory about the justification of *empirical*
beliefs. It appeals to perceptual input and explanatory system.
When we turn to ethical beliefs, we encounter analogues to the
problems with coherence theory in science; the question is whether
there are also analogues to the solutions. Where are the analogues to perceptual input and explanatory system? Or, if there
are no analogues, where are the substitutes that play the same
justificatory role?

Of course, we could resign ourselves to only weak analogies and
so to a more modest interpretation of 'coherence' for ethics. But
the less demanding a requirement coherence represents, the less

improvement in our beliefs reaching coherence will represent, and, at the extreme, there must sometime come a point at which the improvement is so slight that we should have to stop thinking of ourselves as involved in anything worth calling 'justification'.

Is there any analogue in ethics to perceptual beliefs? Are there beliefs of high reliability, beliefs of a credibility to some extent independent of their relation to other beliefs? Might the core values that Wittgenstein and Davidson speak of, the values that are part of the framework for intelligibility, be all the highly reliable beliefs that ethics needs? I doubt it. They may be all that ethics has, but they will not get us far. They will be confined, I take it, to a few basic prudential values—for instance, that we want to avoid pain and anxiety, that we have aspirations and attach importance to their being fulfilled—and perhaps also a few basic moral beliefs—for instance, that cruelty is wrong, and that we must show respect of some sort for others. But we shall have nothing comparable to the rich set of observations that operate in justifying scientific beliefs. Those few unshakeable prudential and moral beliefs will do no more than rule out the craziest of moral theories. The notion of respect, it is true, is closely connected to more specific concepts, such as some form of loyalty and honesty, but even their addition does not provide much of a test. It could not effectively test the moral views that we now think of as seriously in contention. Those views share most of the same specific ethical concepts; they differ over where in deliberation these concepts figure.[23]

There are various ways of enlarging the set of core beliefs necessary for intelligibility. They are by no means confined to ethical beliefs. Our core values are part of our being able to see others as persons; they are normative constraints on central notions in the philosophy of mind.[24] To see an event as an action, one must be able to see it as intentional, which requires seeing it as aimed at some good or other. But these mental notions are involved in the claims about intelligibility that we have already made.

One might also try adding to the core beliefs various specific ethical notions—what are now often called 'thick' concepts—such as 'loyal', 'honest', 'just', 'chaste', 'patriotic', and so on. If they are not quite part of what Wittgenstein calls our form of life, they are anyway much more deeply embedded in a culture, indeed in a particular period of a culture, than thin terms such as 'good' and 'ought'. But thickness is not reliability. Our thick concepts largely define our current common-sense ethical outlook. They are many of the intuitions that I spoke of at the start. They are not the highly reliable beliefs that we hope might be available.

Might we find such beliefs, then, in a different way? We could, as some philosophers suggest,[25] put intuitions through an initial sifting, looking for coherence not with all our moral beliefs, no matter how confused or ephemeral, but only with 'considered' ones. My considered intuitions, I could say, following John Rawls's lead, are those of which I am confident for a fair amount of the time and which I formed in the absence of conditions likely to corrupt judgement—for example, I was calm, adequately informed, and my self-interest was not aroused.[26] 'Considered' judgements would seem, then, to have more weight than unsifted intuitions, and so coherence with them would be more likely to bring improvement.

With perceptual beliefs, we have reason to think that we are to some extent passive recipients of an independent reality. Part of what enters the holistic balance in science is an account of what goes on in observation, because that is part of what is to be explained. We test our beliefs about how we are causally connected to what we observe, how we make perceptual errors and correct them. In the natural sciences, part of what is being justified holistically is our belief in there being certain sorts of reliable beliefs. And it receives a lot of justification at quite early stages in our thought about the world, without our needing much help from philosophy—from, say, epistemology and metaphysics. We know that if our eyes and the light are good, and we are close up, and we take a good look, our resultant belief about what we see is especially secure. With considered judgements in ethics we have nothing like as strong an assurance. This is the central point in the case against piecemeal appeal to intuitions. The causal story of our ethical beliefs is generally much more tangled, much less easily established, than the story of our perceptual beliefs. Perhaps *some* value judgements are perception-like, and the causal story behind them is relatively simple. There is a lot to be said for that view, I think, in the case of prudential value judgements, judgements about what meets or fails to meet basic human interests.[27] But complex moral norms—norms, say, about stealing or killing—have highly complex causes.[28] Some of them arise from solutions to co-operation problems that evolve in a society well below the level of conscious decision. Social convergence, convention, myths, taboos, religion, metaphysics, light or dark pictures of human nature, economic conditions, and so on play an important role. And this highly complex causal background makes ethical beliefs more susceptible to defects. This is not to deny that we can supply a causal account of our normative ethical beliefs or an error theory for them. But neither will be forthcoming until we are able to answer certain metaethical questions in a certain way. Nor is it to deny that most of us must quite naturally get a fair amount right in our ethical beliefs, and that those sound beliefs constitute a basis for criticizing our ethical beliefs generally. But it is to deny that those beliefs constitute anything like as large or as identifiable a group as do the highly reliable beliefs in the natural sciences. This difference between them is, it is true, only a difference in degree, but a difference in degree can turn into a big difference in how rich an interpretation the notion of 'coherence' will bear and in how powerful the coherence test will be. In any case, we cannot know what to expect until we know more about the nature of prudential values and of moral norms, and that means broaching some of the central issues in metaethics. Perhaps some value judgements are perception-like, but we need good (metaethical) reasons to accept that conclusion. It is hard to confine the question of justification within the boundaries of normative ethics.

Nor, I should say, is there a strong analogue in ethics to science's goal of an explanatory system. We have a much better idea how to measure the success, and so the correctness, of some set of beliefs if we know what our purpose in forming them is. We know about standards of success for a natural science: does it describe how its chosen part of the world works? The natural world, as we grasp it, is a network of causes, and this conception of it tends to make our description of it systematic. What, then, is our aim in holding ethical beliefs? The general answer is plain enough: to decide how to live. But there is nothing in that aim that need take us far down the road to either explanation or system. To decide how to live, we need prudential and moral standards. But they might arise in a piecemeal, unsystematic way. Some of them, as I have just suggested, probably embody solutions to co-operation problems, with different solutions to the same problem evolving in different societies and solutions to different problems evolving in a single society largely in isolation from one another. The aim of deciding how to live is achieved, in this part of life, once we have tolerably satisfactory solutions to these co-operation problems; not much in the way of system and explanation is required. Our ethical and other beliefs, it is true, do support one another up to a point; it would be an exceptional ethical belief that did not stand in an inferential or evidential relation to other beliefs. There is doubtless some degree of organization to our ethical thought. But that is far from these beliefs' forming, as our scientific beliefs do, a systematic network of credibility transfers. It is hard to see why they should. It is not enough that our ethical principles themselves should form a system in the familiar sense that they be organizable into a structure—of subordination, for instance (as in utilitarianism all secondary principles are subordinate to the single principle of utility), or of equipollence (as in W. D. Ross's intuitionism the seven prima-facie duties are same-level principles). The sort of system that we are looking for now is one not simply of organization into a structure but of organization into a network of credibility transfers that can raise the level of the whole set of beliefs. The first sort of system can lead to the second, but it need not.[29] I am not saying that we can tell, at this early stage, that no system in the second, stronger sense will emerge between ethical beliefs; what I am suggesting is that, at this stage, we have no reason to assume that it will. Nor is it enough that our ethical beliefs should display system in another familiar sense—that a general principle should throw light on particular cases, often quite difficult ones, and vice versa. This certainly happens—in fact, a bit too readily for it to show much. Utilitarians rightly think that the principle of utility illuminates very many particular cases; deontologists rightly think that the principle of respect for persons, or the doctrine of double effect, does too; and so on. I suspect that it is most often this sort of mutual illumination that philosophers have at the back of their minds when they hold that ethics is capable of system. But achieving this sort of system does nothing to discriminate between major moral views. A view would not have become major, I suppose, unless it had a good deal of this power. But the explanatory circle is too small. Not much in the way of credibility transfers will flow along these short lines.

6. *What we need*

What we should do, then, is to start more modestly—not in order to embark on a Cartesian reconstruction of the whole body of our ethical beliefs, which is neither a modest nor a feasible project, but in order to start more or less where these reasonable, non-Cartesian doubts actually leave us. We should not even assume that 'justification'—that is, some integrated structure of credibility transfers—is appropriate to ethics. There are certainly transfers of credibility between beliefs in ethics here and there, and the local networks of transfers may sometimes become quite extensive. But we should not assume that it is a philosopher's job to find a global network for ethics, on the model of the competing theories of justification for empirical beliefs. What we are after is something that does not require these strong assumptions: namely, some sense of our critical powers in ethics, some idea of how, and how far, we can improve our ethical beliefs.

To that end, there are two things that we can do. First, we can look for beliefs of high reliability, either high relative to our other beliefs or high on some absolute scale of security of beliefs. Our criticism of our ethical beliefs would be advanced even by having to accommodate beliefs of relatively high reliability, but it would be advanced still more if the beliefs were of absolutely high reliability. If, as I suspect, ethical beliefs of high reliability are not confined to those core beliefs necessary for intelligibility, then we must find out what these further beliefs are. Even without beliefs of high reliability, achieving coherence on a wide front provides a test the passing of which confers at least some credit on a set of beliefs. But because of the freedom we should have in arriving at coherence, the credit might be quite modest. A lot would turn on how respectable our initial set of ethical, and other, beliefs happened to be. I include 'other' beliefs because, clearly, it is not just ethical beliefs that can count for or against ethical beliefs; one might include in the final coherence any belief relevant to any ethical view.[30] If this large set were fairly respectable, achieving coherence could bring considerable improvement. If it were not, then it might well bring little. But I myself should not know what achieving coherence in my own case brought unless I knew something about the respectability of my own initial beliefs. It might, of course, boost my confidence in where I ended up if I found that others were ending up there too. But this is another way in which ethical belief differs importantly from empirical belief. Convergence in belief boosts confidence only if the best explanation of the convergence is of the right sort. With a perceptual belief, if mine differs from everyone else's, the best explanation is that my sense is malfunctioning; if it converges, I can be reassured. It is much less clear what the best explanation of convergence in ethical belief is (think, for instance, of the various convergences we have today), and so how reassuring it is. We should have to know how reliable and how decisive some of the beliefs entering the convergence are. Of course, convergence helps—I shall rely on its help later on[31]—but for it to do so, we also need a fair amount of confidence that it is happening for the right reasons. Can we have that confidence without settling major questions in metaethics? Can we have it without finding some beliefs of high reliability? It may be that there is no stronger test available to us than coherence without beliefs of high reliability; but we should not resign ourselves to the modesty of our critical powers until we are pretty sure we must.[32]

The second thing that we can do is to get a better idea of what ethics can reasonably aspire to be. Can it, for instance, aspire to system? We can do this in part by asking what agents would have to be like to be able to live the sort of life that various systematic ethics demand of them.

Both these projects, especially the first, require broaching some central issues in metaethics.[33] To my mind, metaethics is not prior to normative ethics; neither can be pursued fruitfully for long without attending to the other. If they are to advance, they will have to advance together.[34]

II

THE GOOD LIFE

1. *The heterogeneity of values*

We philosophers tend to assume that value judgements are homogeneous, that by and large what holds of one holds of all. But it
would be better at the start to assume the opposite. The status of
the standards that we use to assess an individual life may be quite
different from that of most moral standards, and moral standards
may differ a lot among themselves.

So we should, at the start of the search for highly reliable ethical beliefs, choose one kind of standard to concentrate on, and
later, when we come to others, keep an open mind about how like
one another they may prove to be. I shall start with prudential
values. I use 'prudence' here in the philosophers' special broad
sense, in which it has to do with everything that makes a life good
simply for the person living it. I start with the prudential case for
two reasons. First, it seems to me a bit easier than the moral one,
while still raising all the central metaethical questions—easier, I
think, even though it is impossible to make a sharp cut between
prudence and morals.[1] And second, human interests hold a particularly basic place among values generally; they get us into the
subject not only a little more easily, but also at an especially deep
point.

2. *Two models of value judgements*

Suppose I am struck by the thought that your life is worthwhile
in a way that my own is not.[2] You are accomplishing things with
your life, let us say, that strike me as giving it a point or a weight
that mine lacks. I might not understand exactly why. Clearly, not
just any achievement of yours would contribute much weight:
flag-pole sitting, even of Guinness-Book-of-Records duration, would

not. For something to contribute weight, it would have to be more than bare, even rare, achievement; it would have to be the achievement of something that is itself valuable. But that would not be quite enough either. The flag-pole sitter might give some people mild, momentary amusement, but such amusement, though not nothing on the value scale, lacks the sort of importance to give life point or weight. And 'accomplishment' (if I may simply take over that word for what I am after) should not be confused with public admiration for one's achievements; the public often admires worthless things, and if accomplishment has a value, it is different from the pleasure of being admired. And so on.

The fairly lengthy definitional exercise I should have embarked upon seems to me to consist of two parts. First, I should have to bring into focus the candidate for value status, largely by distinguishing it from other values and from the valueless. Then I should have to decide whether accomplishment, finally seen plainly, is indeed valuable. This exercise looks like, and in some sense is, a process of discovery, and it looks as if the value discovered is valuable quite apart from my personal desires and inclinations—indeed, is valuable for humans generally. And accomplishment is not in this respect a special case. The same seems true of many central prudential values: deep personal relations, contact with important features of reality, living autonomously. These cases all seem to fit what we might call the perception model. The perception model gives priority to a judgement of value: desired *because* valuable. That is, we recognize something to be valuable, and therefore form a desire for it.

Other cases, however, look rather different. They seem to rest far less on our perception or understanding, and more on our individual desires and inclinations. Enjoyment is an obvious prudential value, and what each of us enjoys is closely connected to what each spontaneously wants or is motivated to get. And what one of us enjoys is often very different from what another enjoys. This case seems to fit what we might call the taste model. The taste model reverses the priority: valuable *because* desired. That is, given the sort of biological and psychological creatures we are, our desires come to fix on certain objects, which thereby acquire value.

The taste and the perception models do not exhaust the field. To reject the one is not necessarily to adopt the other. For instance, one might instead think that there is no priority between value and desire. And one might think that the distinction between desire and understanding that both models rely on is too sharp

3. Which model?

There are various ways of bringing those different cases under a single explanation. David Hume, for instance, thought that, despite first appearances, all cases really fit under the taste model. Many who disagree with him about moral standards agree at least about prudential ones. That position seems to me typical of current thought: reject the taste model for moral standards, but retain it for prudential ones. The taste model, with that restriction on its scope, is now widespread in philosophy, and, even without the restriction, dominates the social sciences.[3]

According to the taste model, desire fixes on an object, which thereby becomes valuable. But what relevance have peoples' *actual* desires to what is in their *interest*? One of the discouraging facts of life is that one can get what one actually wants only to find that one is not better off, and sometimes even worse off. Economists are interested in *actual* desires and preferences, I think, for two reasons. First, actual desires are appropriate to some empirical theories of behaviour, but we are now interested in the more normative matter of the quality of life. Second, satisfying actual desires avoids the taint of paternalism; it grants 'consumer sovereignty'. But we must not confuse respect for autonomy with concern for quality of life; what promotes the one may not promote the other.

In the face of the irrelevance of *actual* desires, the common move is to shift to *rational* (or *corrected* or *informed*) desires. It is not that everything that we desire is thereby valuable; our desires can be based on false belief or on incomplete acquaintance. For instance, one might be happy-go-lucky and not want to accomplish anything with one's life. Then one might embark on the train of thought I just sketched, in the course of which one might spend much time bringing the possible value that I christened 'accomplishment' into focus. But once the object is in focus, it will, according to the taste model, owe its status as a value to its then being desired. This explains, one might suggest, the appearance of discovery that this case often presents; in a sense the value is discovered, but understanding comes in merely to bring the natural world into clearer focus, while desire, if it follows, is what transforms the object focused upon into a value. In general, what is valuable to a person is what the person desires when sufficiently informed about the natural world. This Humean development of the taste model offers a simple picture: a natural world, including humans and their responses, exhausting reality; values not being a further element of reality but, rather, created by humans' reacting approvingly to an element of reality when they are aware of its relevant features.[4]

But the taste model, even in Hume's sensitive hands, must be too simple. There are three considerations, not independent of one another, that complicate it. First, the model does not make the standards for a desire's being 'rational' strong enough to explain value. If value can be explained in terms of desire at all, we are now saying, it can be only in terms of rational, not actual, desire. But 'rational' in what sense? Suppose we say that my desire is rational if it exists when I am aware of the relevant natural facts and in the absence of logical error.[5] But a particularly irrational desire—say, one planted deep when one was young—might well survive criticism by facts and logic, and its mere endurance is less than it takes for its fulfilment to make one better off. For instance, I might always wish to hog the limelight and have learned from long experience, perhaps even learned deeply from years of psychoanalysis, how this harms my life. But I might, none the less, still want to hog it. I might not react appropriately, or strongly enough, to what I have learned. Or take a man with some crazy aim in life—say, counting the blades of grass in various lawns.[6] He accepts that no one is interested in the results, that the information is of no use, and so on. He makes no logical error. But it is very unlikely that we can see the fulfilment of this obsessive desire as enhancing his life—apart, that is, from preventing anxieties or tensions that might be set up by frustrating the desire. But anxiety and tension are not the point; we all recognize them as undesirable. What is hard is to see the fulfilment of the crazy desire as, in itself, improving the quality of his life. But again, this makes it doubtful that our standard of 'rational' has become tough enough yet. To make it tougher, though, we should have to make desires 'rational' in some such strong sense as 'formed in proper appreciation of the nature of their object'. But this further demotes the importance of the mere fact of a desire's fixing on an object, and promotes instead the importance of our responding appropriately to it. The mere fact that the term 'rational desire' still retains the word 'desire' does not show that much, or any, of the taste model is surviving. The taste model has no ready answer to the question, When is a response appropriate? One cannot answer that the appropriate response is the 'natural' or 'normal' one. If 'normal' here means 'most common', then we sometimes find that most of us, even when informed, go on wanting certain things—say, self-assertion—too much. If 'normal' is taken to mean something closer to 'correct', then that is just the stronger standard we are trying to explain. In any case, there is something more than a majority response to appeal to: certain responses just are appropriate to certain things, such as living a life of point or weight. Another way of putting this is that the taste model supplies no adequate account of progress in prudential deliberation.

Hume's own account in his essay 'On the Standard of Taste' does not do it. He imagines a young man who prefers the amorous, tender images of Ovid and an old man who prefers the wise reflections of Tacitus.[7] What is clear is that tastes and sentiments, as such, have none of the authority that we attach to values. That is, the mere fact that my feelings prompt me to approval or disapproval would, in fact, cut no ice, even with me, unless I could sort my feelings into better and worse, sound and unsound. But then Hume's point is that tastes and attitudes can improve; we accept some as more refined, sensitive, and subtle than others. Perhaps there is such a thing as 'a best possible set' of them— namely, the limiting set for tastes and attitudes having gone through all improvement. We might say of the old man and the young man in Hume's example that their sensibilities become better if each recognizes and gives weight to the sensibility of the other. In this case, perhaps, the better sensibility is one that incorporates both, and regards Ovid and Tacitus as of equal merit. Divergence in evaluation is prima-facie reason to believe that it is wrong to maintain either of the conflicting attitudes to the exclusion of the other; it gives us occasion to turn two partial perspectives into a more complete one. It may, for example, find them of equal merit (as with Ovid and Tacitus), or one better than the other, or of such different merits that ranking is impossible, and so on.

Widening our sensibility may end up in any one of several quite different places.

It is true, of course, that any of these various resolutions is possible. But what determines which we accept? The whole process of assessment, the whole mode of deliberation that is supposed to be available to us here, is left completely undescribed, and the important questions about the criticism of tastes and attitudes are not answered, but ignored. When we face an attitude that diverges from our own and, at Hume's prompting, open our eyes to this alien sensibility, do our attitudes then just change, as a matter of brute psychological fact, and therefore become better? But what if they do not change? Or change differently for different persons? And why should this be not just change, but improvement? The questions need answers, and it is not clear what Hume's answers would be.[8]

My second point against the taste model is this. It is not that no one has answers; there are the makings of an answer in the sort of prudential deliberation that seems to be within our reach. According to Hume, for a desire to improve is for it to change in content as a result of greater knowledge of the natural world. Desires are fully improved when knowledge of the relevant natural facts is as full as possible; there is then no further scope for criticizing each person's subjective set of desires.[9] But there does seem to be further scope. If certain desires happen not to be present in a final subjective set of improved desires, perhaps they ought to be. And there are forms of deliberation that seem to lead to their introduction. The subjective set that is supposed to be final on Hume's version of the taste model seems not to be really final. We ask more searching questions about our aims, and resort to more radical criticism to answer them, than the taste model allows. If I am a fool-like person living for day-to-day pleasures and meet a Socratic sort who strikes me as making something of his life, I might start on the radical reflection I outlined earlier. Does accomplishing something with one's life make it prudentially better? What is accomplishment? I should then be embarked on the search for the definition of the possible value. I should have to use value-rich vocabulary to bring it into focus: accomplishment is roughly the achievement of the sort of value that gives life weight and point. But then, having isolated it, I should have to decide whether the apparent value is really a value; or rather, since the search for a definition already brings in value-rich language, these two processes—definition of the putative value and decision about its value—go hand in hand. And one decides whether it is a value not by appeal to one's final subjective set of desires. There is nothing there to appeal to, except the vacuous desire to have a good life, which will not do the job, because the present job is to decide whether accomplishment, so defined, makes a life good. So the final subjective set of desires that you or I happen to end up with seems to play no real role here, while understanding what accomplishment is seems to be playing a large role. This sort of understanding, which has its own standards for success, might therefore introduce a new item into one's set of desires in a way that the taste model does not explain. Much more should be said about this sort of understanding and its standards of success, and I shall come back to it in Chapter IV.

To turn now to my final point, the taste model assumes that we can isolate valued objects in purely natural terms and then, inde-pendently, react to them with approval or disapproval. But can we? Prudential deliberation about accomplishment is not a case of first perceiving facts neutrally and then desire's entering and happening to fix on one object or other. The act of isolating the objects we value is far from neutral.[10] We bring what I am calling 'accomplishment' into focus only by resorting to such terms as 'giving life weight or point', and such language already organizes our experience by selecting what we see favourably. Desire is not left free to happen to fix on one object or another; its direction is already fixed in, and manifested by, what we see favourably. It is not that understanding is now dominant and desire subordin-ate; it is not that the order in the taste model (valued because desired) is simply reversed. It is doubtful that we can fully explain the sort of understanding at work in this case—that is, the sort that involves fixing on certain objects and seeing them in a favour-able light—without introducing certain volitional elements. There is no adequate explanation of their being *desirability* features with-out appeal to certain natural human motivations. To see some-thing as an accomplishment leaves no space for desire to follow along in a separate, subordinate position. One cannot here distin-guish the identification of the object to be responded to and the response to it.

Does that matter? Perhaps the taste model does not require us to pick out the class of 'accomplishments', or any other class of values, solely in natural terms. Perhaps we cannot. Our language may often lack the vocabulary that would allow us to delineate the extension of certain value terms solely in natural predicates. That lack may sometimes not even be remediable. For example, 'funny' is a term of assessment, and it is plausible that the only way to pick out the class of funny things is by appeal to the characteristic human reaction to them. We may be able to give natural descriptions only of the various subclasses of funny things and then learn to group those subclasses under the single predicate 'funny' by appeal to that reaction. But why, an advocate of the taste model might ask, is any of this damaging to the model?[11]

It is damaging, I think, because the taste model must still claim that we can pick out in purely natural terms what we react to; it must claim that, though we may not be able to pick out the whole class, we can pick out at least subclasses or individuals, and that our reaction to them will then serve to collect them together into the whole class. But that seems not always to be so. It may be so with 'funny', because the reaction in question is specific to the class of funny things: namely, being amused. The reaction in question with a concept like 'accomplishment' is usually taken to be the highly generic one of approval. But such a generic reaction cannot be used to draw various individuals or subclasses into the class of 'accomplishments', because we react with approval to a great deal more than simply to accomplishments. And if we look for a less generic reaction in this case, then, in order to do the job, the reaction would have to be one of finding that something gives life weight or point. Accomplishments, you will recall, differ from mere achievements—that is, using these words as the terms of art I have turned them into—simply because they give life weight or point, so that is the feature needed to explain our grasp of the concept. But finding that something gives life weight or point seems more a judgement about it than a reaction to it. What the taste model means by reactions are feelings: such generic ones as approval or attraction, and perhaps more specific moral feelings such as guilt, shame, resentment, and gratitude. And our finding that something gives life weight or point seems to fall well outside that range of moral feelings. In any case, it is doubtful that even the relevant subclasses can themselves be picked out in purely natural terms. Darwin accomplished great things in the course of his life. He gave us understanding of important matters;

that was the form that his particular accomplishment took. However, the terms 'understanding' and, even more so, 'important' are probably barred from what a Humean would consider a purely natural description. Yet, without them, the subclass would not be what we react to positively. More needs to be said about this, and I shall come back to it in the next chapter. The taste model gives clear priority to desire over value. But when one looks at the details of prudential deliberation, it is hard to find a priority to either. This leaves the relation of desire and understanding in need of a lot of explanation. But whatever the final explanation, it seems doubtful to me that it could be anything as simple as the taste model would have it.

The final explanation will have to give a smaller role to personal reaction and feeling. For me to see anything as prudentially valuable, I must see it as enhancing life in a generally intelligible way, in a way that pertains to *human* life, not to any one particular person's life. Why should this be so? It runs counter to widespread belief. One reason why we resist this conclusion is that it seems to fly in the face of plain facts about the very different things that people get out of life. I shall come to that in a moment. Another reason is that we tend to overlook the constraints that are part of the constitution of desires. There are different sorts of desires. Some desires are, in effect, afflictions: cravings, obsessions, compulsions, post-hypnotic suggestions, addictions, habits. We passively observe their occurrence in us. But there are also desires that are part of normal intentional action. We have options; we reflect, choose, and act. Desires of this sort aim at the good: an agent's normal behaviour is to recognize interests and to act to meet them.[12] This sort of desire fails on its own terms if it does not aim at something that seems good; it essentially involves a judgement of good, or at any rate some primitive form of one.[13]

It may look as if I am over-generalizing, overdoing a good point. Perhaps most things are valuable only because they are subsumable under some general human interest. Perhaps all the values that I have talked about so far are like that: pleasure, accomplishment, understanding. Call them 'impersonal values'. But surely some are not; some have weight only in particular persons' lives, such as rock climbing or playing the piano well. Some are valuable only from a particular person's point of view: they are what that person cares about. Call them 'personal values'.[14]

But it is doubtful that there are any such things as personal values, in this sense (there are, of course, things that are valuable to only a few people, but that is different). A very odd person might care a lot about counting the blades of grass in various lawns, but that does nothing to make it valuable. And this point does not depend upon his being odd. The same applies to a train-spotter or a piano-player. For anyone to see anything as valuable, from any point of view, requires being able to see it as worth wanting. This is a perfectly general requirement on values; it is the basis of the distinction between mere wanting and the sort of wanting that connects with values. One way to see something as worth wanting is to see it under the heading of some general human interest. Anyone who thinks that not all values are like that must then explain in what further way we can see them as worth wanting. What could make playing the piano well worth wanting is that it would be in some way rewarding: I should enjoy it, or it would be an accomplishment, and so on. But this is to fall back on impersonal values. So long as one defines 'personal values' in terms of what a person wants or cares about,[15] one retains too much of the taste model.

Perhaps playing the piano well is a bad example. A better—perhaps the best—example is how valuable one individual can be to another. It is undeniable that my children are vastly more important to me than they are to strangers, and that this fact can be given at least some sort of explanation by appeal to a class of personal values. But nothing is valuable, or a reason for action, simply by my caring about it. The general requirement stands: I have to be able to see my children's welfare as worthy of concern. And of course it is, for reasons most naturally explained by appeal to impersonal values. Of course their welfare matters—does not everyone's? That explains why it is worthy of respect. But what explains why *their* flourishing is of great importance *to me*, while the flourishing of most others is not? The answer to that is also obvious: I love them, and I do not feel the same way about the rest of humanity. My love explains why I care so much about their flourishing, why it becomes one of the main aims of my life. But it does not explain why it is a great *value* in the first place, why its achievement will make either my life or theirs more valuable.

Still, something that the distinction between personal and impersonal values is getting at is undeniably important. Though I care about my children vastly more than I do about strangers, I do not doubt that everyone matters, and matters equally. I cannot see how I could explain to you why, in the general scheme of things, my child matters any more than yours. And these two concerns of mine—for my child and for fairness—conflict. And the conflict lies at the heart of ethics: a good life is a life of deep commitments to particular persons, institutions, and causes, but a moral life must be a life of fairness between all people. To my mind, though, it is much more helpful to see this not as a conflict between different kinds of values, but rather as a conflict between different concerns and motivations. The conflict leaves us with the major question, How can we manage to live a reasonably integrated moral life?[16] The demands of equal respect for persons threaten to turn ethics into a matter of ferocious, quite unrealizable impartiality between people, swamping all personal concerns. If we are to have an integrated moral life, then we shall have to find a counterweight to impersonal values. It is natural to think that the counterweight could only be some further kind of value— personal values—but that seems to me a mistake. It is better to look not to personal values, but to the nature of a prudentially good life and the nature of agents. That is altogether too laconic a proposal to be clear, but I shall expand it throughout much of the rest of this book.[17]

4. A general profile of prudential values

To see anything as prudentially valuable, then, we must see it as an instance of something generally intelligible as valuable and, furthermore, as valuable for any (normal) human. Prudential deliberation ends up, I think, with a list of values. Let me, for illustration, use my own list; it is no doubt incomplete, and will anyway need revision when later we give up the over-sharp distinction between prudence and morality that I am using now.

(a) *Accomplishment.* I have already spoken about this.

(b) *The components of human existence.* Choosing one's own course through life, making something of it according to one's own lights, is at the heart of what it is to lead a human existence. And we value what makes life human over and above what makes it happy. What makes life 'human' in the special normative sense that the word has here centres on 'agency'. One component of agency is deciding for oneself. Even if I constantly made a mess of my life, even if you could do better if you took charge, I would not let you do it. Autonomy has a value of its own. Another component is having the basic capabilities that enable one to act: limbs and senses that work, the minimum material goods to keep body and soul together, freedom from great pain and anxiety. Another component is liberty: the freedom to read and to listen to others, the absence of obstacles to action in those areas of our life that are the essential manifestations of our humanity—our speech, worship, and associations.

(c) *Understanding.* This, too, I have spoken about a little. Simply knowing about oneself and one's place in the world—certain important anthropocentric knowledge—is part of a good life. We value, not as an instrument but for itself, the authenticity of our experience, life free from illusion and delusion.

(d) *Enjoyment.* We value pleasures, the perception of beauty, the enjoyment of the day-to-day textures of life.

(e) *Deep personal relations.* When personal relations become deep, reciprocal relations of friendship and love, then they have a value apart from the pleasure and profit they bring.

It does not matter if you disagree with my list.[18] I have wanted merely to give reasons for thinking that prudential deliberation would end up with a general profile of values, a chart to the various high points that human life can rise to, if not quite this one, then another.[19] We all, with experience, build up such a profile of the components of a valuable life, including their relative importance. These values, if our profile is complete, cover the whole domain of prudential values.

5. *Individual differences*

My talk about a general profile of values, as I have admitted, seems to deny plain facts about the different things that people get out of life. But so far as I can see, it is, on the contrary, consistent with all such facts.

The values on the profile are valuable in any life. Individual differences matter, not to the content of the profile, but to how, or how much, or even whether, a particular person can realize one or other particular value. But then they matter a great deal. We also learn how individuals deviate from the norm. For instance, I may find accomplishment anxiety-making, and so I face, as you do not, an unlucky clash of values. Or, being ebullient, you may enjoy things more than most persons, whereas I am depressed and enjoy nothing very much. Also the form that a value takes in different lives is bound to vary: what you can accomplish, or enjoy, in your life may well be different from what I can in mine. You may value trekking in the Himalayas, while I may value staying put in a hammock in my garden; and neither of us may value the other's pursuit. Still, it remains true that both our pursuits are valuable only because they fit under some such heading as 'enjoyment'. All this reasoning about individual differences takes place within the framework of a set of values that applies to everyone.

This holds even of the sorts of values that the taste model fits most comfortably. One prudential value is enjoyment, and different persons enjoy different things, or the same things to different degrees. So we get no understanding of how well off a person is in this respect by appealing to a general profile. We have to move on to other grounds: general causal knowledge and information about particular persons. Do you enjoy wine more than I do? I need to know something about your powers of discrimination and your capacity for enjoyment. If I learn that your powers of enjoyment are undulled, that you have a discriminating palate (whereas I do not), and that this wine rewards discrimination, then I have my answer. Still, even with my tastes of the most literal sort, my reasoning often does not focus on me as an individual. I might make my palate as trained as yours. Should I bother? Well, most people with trained palates do not enjoy plonk less, but do enjoy most wines more. For this sort of reasoning I do not need to know what it is like in my particular skin; I need to know what makes life enjoyable and how I am placed to exploit its possibilities.

There being just one profile of prudential values for humans is compatible with there being very many forms that a good human life could take. And because of the importance of autonomy, it is compatible too with respect for considerably less than the best forms of life. Monism about profiles is compatible, to my mind, with all acceptable forms of pluralism.

6. *Dubious dualisms*

This account of prudential deliberation raises doubts about some historically important dualisms in ethics.

(a) *Reason/desire*. Philosophers have often treated the terms 'reason' (or 'cognition', 'understanding', 'perception') on the one side and 'desire' (or 'feeling', 'sentiment', 'passion') on the other, as marking two largely independent manifestations of the human mind. They thus have to explain how reason and desire interact, or should interact, and from the time of Plato they have resorted to political metaphors. Those philosophers of a rational bent (for example, Plato and Kant) assign 'reason' a commanding authority over human life. Others of an anti-theoretical, empirical bent (for example, Hume), rightly suspicious of talk about the dominion of reason, make it the slave of the passions. But these political metaphors hardly do justice to their subject. As we have just seen, when it comes to prudential deliberation, reason and desire are not independent enough for one to be master and the other slave. What is more, it under-describes their true relation to say merely that we need both, without dominance of either, to explain the status of some objects as prudential values. We should also say, more strongly, that the role of neither can, in itself, be properly described without appeal to the other. Desire is not blind: we should regard a totally uninformed desire as without authority, as an affliction that we passively observe but do not associate ourselves with. Reason is not inert: part of the explanation of the status of a practical reason has to bring in connections with human motivation. The correct account of prudential deliberation seems to reject the assumption common to both the taste model and the perception model—namely, that reason and desire are distinct enough for there to be an issue about priority.

Desire, I say, is not blind. I have already suggested that typical desires, desires that are part of intentional action, aim at the good. That they do is not a mere fact about them; it is part of their being such desires. So these desires are not independent of the recognition of the good. The very few desires of which this is not true— say, some baffling urge left by hypnotic suggestion—are only vestigial desires; an urge remains while all the accompaniments that locate it in a natural human life have disappeared. Something similar is true of a whole range of feelings—emotions such as anger and fear, attitudes such as gratitude and resentment. They all essentially involve belief; it is not resentment, say, that one feels unless one believes that one has been treated badly.[20] They are not simple urges either, but part of a much more complex, human way of experiencing the world. Motivation is in this way like perception. We contrast the innocent eye and the intelligent eye, the innocent eye passively registering raw sensory input, what philosophers have called 'sense-data', the intelligent eye interpreting, bringing under concepts. But perception without any interpretation is no perception at all. In that sense, there is only an intelligent eye. Similarly, we might try contrasting the innocent will and the intelligent will, the innocent will being an urge unconnected to any human interest, whereas the intelligent will aims at the good. But if we were beset by mere urges, coming from we know not where and we know not why, inclining us this way and that, we should see them as something to resist, to rid ourselves of as much as we could. They would be for us an alien intrusion, no part of *our* motivation.

And reason, I say, is not inert. What Hume and others find hard to accept is that a cool act of intellection can create anything as warm-blooded as a new motive. But this scepticism depends upon our keeping desire and understanding at a considerable distance from one another. Any normal person who is frittering his life away has a reason to try to accomplish something with it. The more ambitious sort of prudential deliberation that I sketched earlier is what he would have to go through to recognize it as a reason. It neither appeals to some pre-existent member of his personal motivational set, nor is entirely free from desires: the understanding that is needed is a grasp of certain desirability features, and they owe their status as such to normal human desires. Understanding and motivation cannot here be very sharply separated.

The sort of connection between understanding and motivation that I have in mind does not mean that we cannot understand a value-word without ourselves actually accepting the value. That would make the connection altogether too simple. Anthropologists can understand alien values without endorsing them. We can understand value-terms in our own culture without regarding them as naming real values. But that is because we and the anthropologist reject some belief that the so-called value needs. We can understand the word 'chastity' because we can see how, if, say, we thought that there were a God and that some forms of sexual abstinence pleased Him, or that abstinence were good for one's spiritual life, it would be important to be chaste. At the same time, if we reject enough of the background, we reject chastity as a virtue. Still, we do not understand the disvalue term 'pain' unless we understand that, typically, humans want to avoid it or have it alleviated—humans typically, but not every individual human. A few individuals might both know what 'pain' means and not have those typical reactions (say, someone racked by guilt who welcomes pain). I suppose, to take a really far-fetched case, that even a Martian anthropologist might do a pretty good job with grasping what we mean by 'pain', though coming from a species without a nerve in its body, so not itself caring about pain. It is not that everyone who knows how to use the word has the relevant reaction, but that the reaction is part of what must be the primary, unreserved use of the word. All value-terms are used against a background of certain beliefs about the world, and when all those beliefs are in place, the word is used unreservedly. If one believes that it is a human interest to accomplish something in the course of one's life, and one believes that it is possible for us to do things that would count as accomplishments, then one uses the word unreservedly. And certain feelings and inclinations are part of those beliefs about human interests. One should not, though, read too much into this distance between understanding and motivation. The Martian anthropologist will not share our human concerns about pain, but that does not mean that he would not regard our judgements about pain as true, or that he would not see our peculiarly human concerns as concerns. And that a human anthropologist does not share our concerns about, say, chastity, shows that they are not genuinely *human* concerns, only concerns given certain local beliefs.

Still, there is, I think, an important truth behind Hume's position. He holds that a practical reason must be backed by some member of a pre-existent personal motivational set. That seems too strong. But what seems right—and important—is that all reasons have to connect, in a way still to be explained, with human motivation. It is a requirement on a reason that it have a certain role in human life: that it move one to belief or to action. What would a reason for action be like that did not? It would purport to present a ground for action that did not mesh with any natural human concern or response. The closest we might come to one would be an arbitrary divine edict—say, God's commanding Abraham to sacrifice Isaac. But not even that is detached from human concerns and responses. Abraham regarded this as a command just because it came from one who, in his scheme of things, rightly had dominion over him. But a putative reason that really did not mesh with motivation would be too remote from human nature to fit intelligibly under the concept of a practical 'reason'. I do not mean that this requirement holds, individual by individual. A psychopath might understand a moral reason, but be totally unmoved by it. Someone in black despair might recognize some urgent prudential reason, and not care a bit. The requirement is only general: that a practical reason has to mesh with characteristic human motivation. I think that the requirement holds for reasons for belief as well as for reasons for action. The former must mesh with characteristic human motivation to believe. But since this leaves it entirely open what motivates belief (including simply perception of truth), the requirement in this case is not especially restrictive. None the less, accepting this requirement can change our conception of reasons. We have a tendency to think of reasons as transcendent, as commands addressed to a resistant or, at best, neutral human nature, whereas, on the contrary, they are reasons only because they incorporate a movement of the human will.

(b) *Objective/subjective.* Is this account of prudential value 'subjective' or 'objective'? By 'subjective' I mean an account that makes a prudential value depend upon people's desires, and by 'objective' one that makes it independent of their desires. This is, of course, only one of the senses that get attached to these two equivocal terms. 'Objective' is also used to mean, roughly, 'exists independently of human thought, feeling, knowledge, response'. That is, the objective/subjective distinction is also used to mark the divide between realism and non-realism. But the senses that I have proposed are probably the most common ones, and the only ones that I am interested in for the moment (I shall come to the realist use later). Now, this account certainly does not make values depend upon *one* person's desires; they could not intelligibly do so. Values are, on the most plausible account of their link to desire, what one would want if one properly appreciated the object of desire. But, as we have seen, this account shifts importance away from the mere occurrence of desire on to the nature of its object. Desire is left playing very little role, even *many* people's desires. Still, desire reappears in another place. To recognize the nature of the relevant object is to see it under some desirability characterization, such as 'accomplishment' or 'enjoyment'. These desirability characterizations give reasons for action, and those reasons in turn mesh with characteristic human motivation. So what one recognizes embodies some element of human reaction. That, it seems to me, is the element of truth in desire accounts of value; it is not nothing, but it is certainly much less than what a desire account is ordinarily thought to be. Neither 'objective' nor 'subjective', on their present definition, therefore, fits the case comfortably.

Why both these dualisms—and others, such as cognitivism and non-cognitivism, which I shall come to later—look dubious is that they invoke too sharp a distinction between recognition and reaction.[21] The relation of those two is difficult to understand. They seem, from the samples of prudential deliberation we have so far considered, to be clearly connected: reaction gets its direction from recognition; recognition gets its point from reaction. Even to put it this way, though, treats them too separately. Understanding the role of recognition and reaction is central to understanding the reliability of prudential judgements, to deciding whether any is especially reliable. We must go into it more deeply.

III

THE BOUNDARIES OF THE NATURAL WORLD

1. *Conceptual naturalism*

We need to understand better how both recognition and reaction are at work in forming our beliefs about values. If recognition is at work at all, it seems, then values must be the *objects* of recognition. The idea of an 'object' of recognition can be understood in a variety of ways. An obvious way is in the manner of realism: values, as objects of recognition, are independent of human thought and feeling; they exist out there in the world, waiting to be recognized. And one way to take 'being in the world' is in the manner of reductive naturalism: values can be reduced to facts about nature. Let me start here.

What is a reduction? To describe a particular reductive programme tolerably fully, one must know its aim or point. Sometimes the aim of these programmes is a kind of ontological soundness. Suspect entities or properties, which may not even exist, are either eliminated by dissolution into others or legitimated by composition from others, hard though it sometimes is to distinguish elimination from legitimation. Another aim can be epistemological satisfactoriness. Puzzling explanations are either replaced by explanations on a different, clearer level or legitimated by finding bridges between the two levels. Reduction therefore has a built-in bias toward the unpuzzling, which is generally a bias toward physicalism or naturalism. This may seem to be an unchallengeable bias. But we are not always puzzled by what we should be puzzled by. And there is another strategy for dealing with the puzzling besides reduction to the unpuzzling. We may manage to make it unpuzzling on its own level of explanation.

Reduction, of its nature, requires two levels of explanation: for instance, in the case we are interested in, the level of values and the level of natural facts. One thing we should be puzzled by are the boundaries of 'natural fact'. The question of the reduction of values to natural facts is not like that of, say, mental states to brain states. We know fairly well what a physiological state is, but we do not know at all well what falls under a category as grossly defined as the 'natural'. We can define the 'natural' as, roughly, what is explained by the natural sciences;[1] but that merely puts the puzzle back one short step to the boundaries of 'natural science'. Do natural sciences include social sciences, themselves the subject of reductivist ambitions? The best prospects for reducing values to natural facts is to make the category of the natural wide: a natural science, we might say, is any systematic set of empirical regularities. This throws all the burden on to the hardly sharp-edged notion of the 'empirical', and it is there that it seems to me best to leave it. Naturalism can be distinguished from materialism, which is the view that everything is reducible to matter in motion, because the 'empirical' is, at least potentially, more inclusive than the 'material'. G. E. Moore, who struggled for many years over the term 'natural', suggested early on that 'natural' might be understood as 'exists by itself in time'.[2] But this account destroys the distinction between natural and non-natural properties, because a natural property, such as 'yellow', cannot be found on its own in time either. *Properties* in general cannot. Moore thought that some could, such as 'yellow', because he thought that natural properties were actual, substantive constituents of, parts of, the wholes that they are the properties of. But this conception of properties as ingredients that, when they coincide in space and time, constitute the substance of an object, would strike most of us now as implausible. At a later stage, Moore seems to have preferred explaining natural properties as 'independent' and non-natural ones as 'dependent':[3] that is, a natural property, such as 'yellow', may be present in an object independently of what other properties it has, whereas a non-natural property, such as 'good', may not. This shifts the natural/non-natural distinction very close to what is now called the supervenient/non-supervenient distinction, as we shall see shortly. But a property like 'large', even a property like 'yellow', does not seem to be independent of other properties of the object. So I think it best to stick to the account of 'natural' in terms of what 'empirical' explanations are about. The empirical/non-empirical distinction, though not at all sharp, seems to me better than the alternatives. Any thought about reduction or supervenience will, at the start, have to put up with rough, intuitive meanings for terms such as 'natural' and 'empirical', because much of what is at issue is where those lines are best drawn. I shall come back to this later.

If one uses the term broadly, one could call the reduction of value to natural fact 'reductive naturalism'. Now, the rough, intuitive sense of 'natural' that most of us work with is the one Hume uses when, for instance, he proposes that values cannot be derived from facts. In that sense, though, I know of no persuasive form of naturalism. There are also, I think, attractive forms of naturalism, which I shall come to at the end of this chapter, but for the moment I want to concentrate on forms of reductive naturalism.

One form is conceptual naturalism, which claims that value-terms are definable by natural terms.[4] I do not want to spend much time on it, because it does not seem at all promising. It is not that G. E. Moore's famous argument finishes it off; on the contrary, I doubt that his argument works. My doubt is not just that, although Moore sets out to prove something about *properties*, he argues only about *words*.[5] Even on its own ground, as a claim about definition, his argument fails. He argues indirectly: if the word 'good' were definable in the sense that matters (namely, were analysable), we could say something of the form: 'good' means 'x plus y plus z'; however, then the claim 'whatever is x plus y plus z is good' would be a tautology, but it never is. Moore offers, of course, less an argument than a challenge: try it and you will fail. Eventually a few people tried and largely succeeded.[6] One relatively simple proposal was that 'good' has associated with it 'the condition of answering certain interests, which interests are in question being indicated either by the element modifying or the element modified by "good" or by certain features of the context of utterance'.[7] In short, 'good' means 'answers to certain interests'. And this semantic analysis seems to be an analysis in just Moore's prohibited sense. What is more, it looks promisingly naturalist. We should say that a tree had good roots, because roots anchor and feed, and these roots do just that. Such judgements seems to be well within the bounds of the natural world. Now, I think that most nouns that can be modified by 'good' apply to things with a function or role or purpose, and that the modifier 'good' applies when they fulfil the function or play the role or achieve the purpose. That is true not just of 'good roots' but also of 'good parent', and even of the very general moral assessment 'good person'. The semantic setting of interests to be met is, I think, seldom missing. But two things seem to me to stop a naturalist from claiming this definition as vindication. First, the semantic analysis does not entirely succeed. A few nouns modifiable by 'good' apply to things without a function or role or purpose, and there is then no interest being served. A good Roman nose is merely one that has the defining characteristics to a high degree. More damagingly, a prudentially good life is good in a way not analysable in terms of satisfying interests, at any rate not analysable in the proposed canonical form. Even if one can set some of these cases aside as falling outside the scope of the thesis (good Roman noses?) and others as connected with interests in some more remote way still to be explained (prudentially good lives?), this version of naturalism would still not be saved. While what the relevant interest is in the case of good roots may be a fact about the natural world, in the case of a good parent or a good person (in the morally weighted sense of that term) the notion of interest becomes so rich as no longer to stay within the bounds of the natural in the Humean way we are understanding them now.

This seems to me the fate of all naturalist definitions: either they fall short of establishing full criteria for the use of the term, or they occasionally establish something close to full criteria by going beyond the resources of what we now usually think of as the natural world.

2. Substantive naturalism

Much the most interesting forms of naturalism are substantive ones. Instead of claiming that value-terms are synonymous with certain natural terms, they claim merely that certain matters of value in effect come down to certain matters about the natural world. It looks on the surface, they say, as if ethics has its own autonomous subject-matter, but, when we dig deeper, all that it really turns out to be about is facts about the human psyche, say, or about social needs and organization. Values, they say, are composed of natural facts; that may not account for all that we now mean when we talk about values, but it accounts for all that there actually is to values.

Substantive naturalism can, of course, take very many different shapes. A rational-desire account of value, for instance, readily lends itself to a naturalist interpretation. It can be seen as reducing value to the purely psychological matter of what one would want if rational.[8] It needs, as we saw in the last chapter, a rather richer conception of rational than it usually gets, because one can be well informed and still want things—for instance, always to be the centre of attention—that do one harm. But could we not add a little more richness without making those desires fall right outside the natural world?[9] The obvious way to do this is to make the antecedent of the counter-factual a little more ideal than it usually is: if I, who want always to be the centre of attention, had not only all the facts and the correct logic, but also the sensitivity to appreciate the import of some of those facts, then I should not want always to demand attention. But what we crucially need is to have the exercise of that sensitivity spelt out in some detail. I suggested earlier that it involves recognizing a reason for action grounded in one's well-being, that it requires bringing a situation under some concept—enjoyment, accomplishment, and so on—that is generally intelligible as something life-enhancing. Without those elements, one's account would not be rich enough. But, with them, would it any longer be naturalist?

This brings us up against the fuzziness of the notion of the 'natural'. Recognizing something as a reason for action or reason for belief, though it is an event in the natural world, clearly also has a normative element to it, and I doubt that what is now commonly understood as a 'naturalist' or an 'empirical' account of the world includes the recognition of norms of reason. What we need to focus on is the difference between a person's regarding something as a reason for belief or for action and its really being one. The former could appear in empirical explanations of behaviour. The latter, however, involving as it does a normative assessment, probably could not. I put that conclusion cautiously, both because of the fuzziness of the boundary of the natural world and because the natural/non-natural distinction, as it stands now, may be an untenable dualism. In any case, there are important claims that cannot easily be parcelled into either class. So all I want to conclude is that, as the term is now widely used, the sensitivity that we have to explain involves events that fall outside the natural world.[10]

There are any number of other forms of substantive naturalism. Our evaluations are themselves events in the natural world, and it is always illuminating to consider empirical explanations of their origin and growth. Freud suggested that 'ethics must be regarded . . . as a therapeutic effort: as an endeavour to achieve something through the standards imposed by the super-ego which had not been attained by the work of civilization in other ways'—namely, control of the constitutional inclination of humans to be aggressive toward one another.[11] And it is likely that some ethical standards originally arose as solutions, not always conscious, to social co-operation problems. Ethical constraints serve the useful social function of making things go better than they would if natural human failings ran on unchecked. One might think—some philosophers do[12]—that these psychological or sociological explanations become wide-ranging and deep enough to leave nothing more to explain. Just as psychological or sociological explanations of religion may explain it so cogently as to convince us that religion is no more than the entirely natural phenomenon just explained, whatever we thought of it before, the same fate, these philosophers think, befalls ethics. The causal explanation of ethics has a corrosive effect, leaving no non-natural subject in need of separate understanding.

Reductive arguments are strong only if they start with a sufficient appreciation of what it is they have to reduce. And the arguments I have just sketched—and all substantive reductionist arguments, I think—fail that test. It seems to be right that one central and important function of ethical standards is to control our instinctive aggression toward one another. But that and other possible psychological explanations cover only a small part of the ground. We also want to make our life both reasonable and fulfilled. We naturally ask, What would make my life (prudentially) better? And the deliberation that we should find ourselves necessarily involved in cannot plausibly be explained exhaustively in terms of controlling aggression or in any other of the sort of depth-psychological terms that would keep it a reductive explanation. Enough, I hope, was said about this in the last chapter. Similarly, some value judgements clearly have their origins in solutions to co-operation problems; these solutions arise and survive because they make social life go better than it otherwise would. But this sort of sociological explanation could not begin to explain all evaluation. If we reflect a moment on the nature of prudential deliberation—on the resources available to us to decide whether accomplishment, say, or deep personal relations are life-enhancing—the reductive explanation looks superficial, very little in accord with the details of what actually goes on. Most of the issues that concern us in prudential deliberation could not check aggression or solve co-operation problems. They are less psyche-directed or society-directed, more reflective and detached, than these reductive accounts make them. It is true that explanations in terms of controlling aggression or solving co-operation problems are intended primarily for moral judgements, and I oppose them by citing prudential judgements. But this does not matter. We are looking for reductions for values generally, including prudential values, and what is difficult is to find any extension of the psychological or sociological proposals that will fit prudential values. And if one cannot reduce prudential values to natural facts, the project of reducing moral standards becomes altogether more problematic. It runs into the difficulty of the close connections between prudential values (for example, the disvalue of pain) and judgements well on the way to moral judgements (for example, that everyone's pain is a disvalue). This, I think, is a point at which some normative ethics—say, an interest in substantive prudential deliberation—would help metaethics: one would not advance these reductive explanations if one had a keener appreciation of just how much needed explaining.

These forms of substantive naturalism once again raise the problem of the boundaries of the natural world. These explanations employ intentionality, and the intentional may fall outside the bounds of the natural, on some common conceptions of the 'natural'. But even if it does not, these lower-level explanations fail to do all of the genuine explanatory work done on the higher level of values. An essential part of saying that accomplishment is prudentially valuable is to say that we have reason to aim at it, not merely that we do aim at it in certain naturally described circumstances.

Despite the failure of this form of naturalism, one of the deep motive forces propelling it seems to me admirable. Values do not need any world except the ordinary world around us—mainly the world of humans and animals and happenings in their lives. An other-worldly realm of values just produces unnecessary problems about what it could possibly be and how we could learn about it. All that seems to me right. But to defend it, one does not have to adopt a reductive form of naturalism. I shall come back to this later too.

3. *The supervenience relation*

All the same, there is clearly some very intimate connection between values and natural properties. Put vaguely, the relation seems to be one of dependence without reducibility. The most common way nowadays of trying to make that statement a little less vague is to say that values 'supervene' upon natural properties: that is, if objects are the same in all natural properties, they must be the same in value.[13] Supervenience allows the dependence of the higher level of explanation upon the lower without reduction, and the autonomy of the higher level without dualism. That middle course seems to me intuitively right for values. None the less, I doubt that values do supervene upon natural facts.

On the common definition I have just given, supervenience is a weak relation. It concerns only indiscernibility: if one has indiscernibility on the natural level, then, of necessity, one has it on the value level. But the chances are that any difference in value will go along with some difference in natural fact, if only in trivial properties such as when and where it occurs. The relation needs to be tightened.

But how much? It is part of the definition of supervenience, as it stands, that the base properties are specified as to kind, and are of a different kind from the supervening properties. And the specification makes the relation non-tautological: the base properties are not defined as any properties, regardless of type, relevant to something's having the supervening property (for example, in the present case, relevant to being valuable), but as being of one independently specified kind (for example, in the present case, natural properties). But I think that something yet stronger is intended. We do not, in the present case, mean any natural property at all, but only ones that appear in explanatory regularities at the natural level, and those explanatory regularities mention kinds of spatial and temporal relations, but do not refer to such particulars as, say, occurring today and in Parks Road, Oxford. But I think that we have to go somewhat further and add a relevance requirement. When we consider the supervenience of, say, mental states on physical states, a relevance requirement is implicit. We would not accept that mental states supervene (trivially) upon physical states if it happened to turn out that there are always likely to be differences at some deep subatomic level that are irrelevant to differences at the physiological level. Nor would we if it turned out that there are likely to be physiological differences in the epidermis unconnected with what is happening in the brain. In the case of mental states, we consider whether they supervene upon a particular kind of physiological state—namely, brain states. Similarly, we consider whether evolutionary biological explanations supervene upon not just any lower-level natural explanation, but upon microbiological ones. We specify the supervened-upon level in the way we do because we believe that there are certain sorts of connections between it and the supervening level. That is why, in expressing our intuitive notion of supervenience, we use words such as 'dependence', 'underlying', 'consequential property'.[14] Those words express, in rough terms, the sort of connection we have in mind. But this creates a problem for us. How do we specify the base level in the present case? It is the problem alluded to earlier, of the grossness of the class of 'the natural'. What we are interested in is whether values supervene upon not just any natural properties, but some subclass of the natural, a subclass relevant to something's being valuable. Though it is not easy to specify the subclass, I think that we should accept the relevance limitation that it represents. Most moral philosophers do.[15] Accepting this relevance restriction moves supervenience toward, though it does not make it quite as strong as, the 'true in virtue of' relation. The latter relation holds only if truth at the higher level is a function just of truth at the lower level, whereas supervenience requires no more than that there is some function or other.[16]

4. Are values supervenient?

The restriction of lower-level properties to relevant natural ones and of upper-level properties to values, which gives supervenience its interest, also, to my mind, makes it doubtful. Supervenience about values accepts a sharp, hardly uncontentious division between the natural world and the world of values. So the supervenience relation is itself far from metaethically neutral. It shares the assumption of the sharp division with the Humean version of the taste model, and is open to similar objections. As we saw in the last chapter, there is no sharp separation of a natural from an evaluative component in a concept such as 'accomplishment'. And purely natural description is not enough to give the concept a shape, to pick out its extension.

That earlier argument does not yet upset supervenience, though. It shows only that the content of prudential concepts does not respect boundaries between natural fact and value. To deny supervenience is to make a stronger claim. We have, it is true, certain firm intuitions in favour of supervenience. How valuable a thing is *must* depend upon what it is like. If there is a difference in supervening property, how could it *not* show up in a difference in base properties? But this is where the dubiousness of the separation of fact and value, or reason and desire, is crucial. To regard some properties as 'base' suggests that *they* are where it all happens and that valuing is something entirely different—a human response, say, or a rather mysterious epiphenomenon. To contrast a thing's 'value' with 'what it is like' suggests that values have no hand in what it is like. Then, of course, our strong pro-supervenience intuition is easily explainable: things are valuable because, and only because, of what goes on in the (natural) world. But this picture begs the central question: What are the boundaries of the *world* or *reality* or *fact*? Once one has reason to doubt that those boundaries simply coincide with those of the natural world, on our current Humean conception of them, and once one sees how much goes into a value-concept besides the natural (indeed, how relatively unimportant the natural component is compared to the rest), then our pro-supervenience intuition starts to weaken.

But the acid test is: Can we supply difference in prudential value without any difference in relevant natural properties? I think that the answer is unclear. If we could mention *any* natural property to establish a difference, then we could always, though uninterestingly, come up with one. Smith's poetry is a genuine accomplishment; Jones's poetry, just as long, varied, innovative, and so on, is not. But Smith and Jones must at least have written in different-colour ink or in different places. But these differences will not do; we need properties that are 'relevant' in the sense explained earlier. It is the relevance requirement in particular that seems to me to introduce a measure of doubt. A lot that is natural is not relevant, and a lot that is relevant is not natural.

Smith's poetry, let us say, is full of understanding of important matters. That is why it is an accomplishment, and that is the particular sort of accomplishment it is. It would be an accomplishment, I suppose, even if, like Emily Dickinson, he put his poems away in a bureau which, unlike Dickinson's, was never opened. Jones's poetry is not an accomplishment precisely because it lacks those qualities: understanding of important matters. The crucial base properties in these cases are *understanding* and *importance*. Yet neither of them fits at all comfortably inside the class of the 'natural', on our Humean interpretation, so in our present sense they cannot be 'base' properties. Must there be some relevant natural differences between the cases none the less? The particular words that Smith and Jones will have used will have been different. But is this any more relevant than the colour of their ink? Admittedly, there is a much closer relation between words and sense than between colour of ink and sense, and a poem's sense connects with its being full of understanding. But the particular words that Smith chose need not have been essential; the sense could have been, and in other drafts may have been, conveyed in different words. So is that, after all, a relevant difference? There is a question, I think, not only about the relevant/non-relevant distinction but also about the natural/non-natural one. On which side of the boundary should epistemological states, such as understanding, come? There is understanding in Smith's case but not in Jones's. But will understanding, with its requirement that norms be met, fall inside the class of the 'natural'? And will the understanding's being important, with that further norm to be met, fall inside it as well?

To my mind, the answers to those questions are not clear, and not clear for a particular reason: the various key distinctions on which the questions turn themselves run out of the sharpness that the answers need. We could certainly make them sharper, and thereby defend the supervenience of values. We could drop the relevance requirement, and allow base properties to be 'base' in a much weaker sense of the word. But then supervenience would be a much less interesting relation.

Supervenience seemed a safe fall-back position for those of us who reject reduction. If values are not reducible to facts, they are, it seems safe to say, at least dependent upon them in the thoroughgoing way that supervenience defines. But what is common to both reduction and supervenience is that they assume a sort of separation of fact and value that does not exist. Values are indeed deeply embedded in facts, but embedded in a way that makes talk of 'dependence' inappropriate.

I am inclined to draw the following moral from these doubts about supervenience. To put it at its most general, prudential values have to do with the world's import for humans. We cannot get at the sort of thing that a prudential value is merely by assembling sets of facts about the natural world, in the fairly narrow sense of 'natural' now widespread in philosophy, because this falls well short of capturing their 'import for humans'. It leaves out what prudential values are about: human interests. That, for instance, is why the person who wanted always to be the centre of attention failed to have rational desires in the strong sense of 'rational' needed to explain values. That, too, is why the *focusing* that, on the taste model, is meant to precede the *reacting* cannot employ only natural facts in this narrow sense; it will not succeed in delineating the appropriate object of the reaction. That is why we need the right value-concepts in order to be fully informed. This is connected with my claim at the end of the last chapter that understanding and desire cannot be kept independent of one another. To understand *import for humans* is to understand *what matters to them*, and so *what is worth their aiming at*. One of the ways in which the concepts in that set are complex is that they apply to points at which understanding and desire merge: what is to be understood *is* how humans, as intentional beings with interests, fare in the world. That is the new subject that the vocabulary of prudential values addresses. It constitutes an ascent from that level of explanation concerned with the world of mechanics and the world of simple organisms, and perhaps even the world of animals with simple interests such as capacity to feel pleasure and pain, to the level of explanation concerned with rational animals, animals capable of deliberation and choice. 'Ascended from' is not the same relation as 'supervenient upon'. It is wider and looser; it probably varies in form from one case to another. It is worth looking at further.

5. *Explanation by ascent*

What I have in mind is a very familiar hierarchy of explanatory theories, with physics at the bottom and an ascent from one level of explanation couched in terms of its particular entities and their interaction to a higher level couched in terms of new entities, in some sense composed of the old ones, and their new forms of interaction. If we do not tie the notion of 'ascent' down too tightly, we can trace an ascent from theories of atomic particles to theories of chemical compounds, and from them to theories of microbiological organisms, and from them to theories of evolution, and so on. One ascends through the hierarchy, because one cannot explain, or explain directly or economically, at the lower level what one can at the higher. The idea of explanation by ascent is capacious enough to include supervenience, but in the case of values at any rate, 'supervenience' does not seem the best way to specify the ascent.

The idea is also extremely rough, and will eventually need a lot of refinement. It is not yet clear how one goes about slicing nature into 'levels', or whether there is only one line of ascent, or in what sense, or perhaps senses, the new entities are 'composed' of the old; or, conversely, in what sense, or senses, the new entities can be 'reduced' to the old. And, more important, it is not clear what the significance of reduction is—when it eliminates entities and when it legitimates them. We need a test for 'existing in its own right'. An intuitively attractive, and perhaps now the most common, test is whether an entity or property must be mentioned in the best explanation of what happens in the world, but the criteria for the 'best' are as yet unclear. For example, we develop causal explanations of behaviour in terms of mental states, but also causal explanations in terms of brain states. The former sort of explanation is the more economical, and it has expressive power that the latter totally lacks. But that is not enough to make it the 'best', and we have to settle what else is needed. What is more, it is hard to tell whether 'ascent' takes us to another theory of the same broad kind—that is, to yet another empirical science— or whether, as Paul Grice has said,[17] it eventually takes us—for example, in the move from an empirical theory of human behaviour to a theory of deliberative agents—out of science and into metaphysics.

These are difficult, ill-defined issues. It may not be possible to say much of a general nature about the relation of lower to higher level, and I shall not try. All that I shall do is to say something about the particular move that concerns us: the ascent to the level at which the closely related notions of agents, interests, and values appear. That will be the subject of the next chapter.

Let me end this chapter with a speculation. Suppose that prudential values—cases of meeting interests—should earn their way into the world of facts. Suppose, that is, that we found a place for them in our everyday world, without resorting to anything remotely like a 'value realm'. That would then be to accept what seems to me immensely plausible about naturalism. In talking about prudential values, we are not talking about entities in such an other-worldly realm—detectable, say, by intuition—but, rather, about certain things that happen in the only realm that values need: mainly, what goes on in human lives, that *this* or *that* meets an interest, and so makes a life go better. It makes sense to ask how these sorts of happenings relate to other, fairly well-defined levels of explanation: say, the psychological. But I doubt that, in the end, there is any point in asking how such happenings relate to a level so grossly defined as the 'natural' or the 'empirical', because the boundaries that we use to delineate the 'natural' or the 'empirical' are not just fuzzy, but so central to what we are now trying to settle as to make assumptions about where they are located question-begging. We do not start our investigations with the boundaries of 'reality', of 'what there is in the world', of the 'empirical', or of the 'natural' already satisfactorily drawn. We have only a common, fuzzy intuition about the 'natural' or 'empirical' world, one that is itself full of contentious ontological assumptions. So we should not start by asking how values connect with the natural or empirical world, as if we really knew the territories in question and wondered only about their foreign relations. That procedure makes their relation more puzzling than it need be. But suppose, as I say, that our notion of 'reality', or of 'fact', or of the 'empirical' is agreed to be wide enough to include events of meeting or failing to meet interests. Then the right position would, after all, be a kind of naturalism. What I spoke against earlier was the familiar sort of reductive naturalism, in which the boundaries of the 'natural' are kept relatively tight: they are kept roughly in the position that they have long had in the traditional fact/value split—for instance, in what I earlier took as Hume's paradigmatic belief that values cannot be derived from facts. What seems attractive, however, is an expansive naturalism in which the boundaries of the 'natural' are pushed outward a bit, in a duly motivated way, with the effect that they now encompass prudential values. (Whether they encompass moral norms is a quite different matter, which I shall come to later.) Values are not reduced; they are swallowed whole. This, I say, is a speculation, but in the next chapter I want to give some reason for taking it seriously.

IV

VALUE AND NATURE

1. *The search for reliability*

The more beliefs of special reliability we have, the greater our critical powers are likely to be.

It is easy to find a few. There are, first of all, the core values that are part of the framework only within which language is possible. But they do not get us far, it seems to me; they rid us of only crazy ethical beliefs, leaving too many plausible-sounding, incompatible ones still around. To the core values, such as the avoidance of pain, we can add accomplishment, understanding, autonomy, and deep personal relations. We can, that is, extend the list of prudential values. But does this also enlarge the pool of especially reliable beliefs?

One reason for suspecting that it does is that these particular non-core values are nearly as deeply embedded in human nature as the core values themselves. We do not understand what a pain is unless we understand how it fits into human life: pains are, among other things, what we want to avoid or to have alleviated. And we do not know what other human beings are unless we know that, typically, they can feel pain. These are parts of the framework necessary for intelligibility. But, similarly, we do not know what other human beings are unless we know that they have desires, which typically aim at the good and can be met or frustrated. People can end up better or worse off over large tracts of their lives. That, too, is part of the necessary conceptual framework. For instance, humans are by nature sociable; they aim at love, affection, or at least company, and lack of these produces its own sorts of pain and malfunction. That truth may not be part of the concept of a human being, but it seems none the less to be a pretty plain fact.

That, I think, is the prima-facie case for expecting some beliefs about non-core values also to be especially reliable. The case is simply that some such values are clear enough features of human nature that to deny them would be a quite plain error. Yet, surprisingly, there are long-standing philosophical doubts about whether value judgements are the sort that can be 'correct' or 'incorrect', 'true' or 'false'.

2. *Can prudential judgements be 'correct'?*

There cannot be any doubt about the correctness of prudential judgements based on biological needs. One absolutely plain human interest is in nourishment; without it we suffer or die. Another plain interest is in certain sorts of human contact; if a baby is fed but receives absolutely no other forms of nurture, it will suffer gross psychological damage. There are clear criteria for the judgements that nourishment and nurture are human interests. One has only to show their link to the avoidance of ailment, pain, or malfunction. The boundaries of these three concepts—ailment, pain, and malfunction—are not sharp, but many cases fall well inside them. Many cases are within the domain of core values. Nourishment and nurture are valuable because they are particular forms of avoiding those core disvalues: ailment, pain, and malfunction.

So let us now move outside the core. One prudential value that I spoke of earlier was deep personal relations. What I meant were relations of love and affection between fairly mature persons, not the nurturing relation between mother and baby. Without deep personal relations an adult will suffer, but it is an altogether less experiential, more contentious sense of 'suffering' than the gross ailment and malfunction in the case of a baby deprived of nurturing. Another prudential value is accomplishment. Whether I accomplish something in my life need not show up in any of my phenomenal states, in the sort of thing that might be introspectible by me or observable by you. That is one reason why I have been giving prominence to the example of accomplishment. To understand prudential values, one has to understand why *it* is one.

Still, these non-core values are both continuous with the core values and, like them, firmly embedded in human nature. Our actions, unless deviant, are intentional; they aim at some good or other. Particularly deeply embedded in us are certain biological aims—for food, health, protection of our capabilities—and certain psycho-biological aims—for company, affection, reproduction. But we are not only intentional; we are also reflective. It does not take us much reflection to see that goods differ in degree, and that they differ in finality (that is, some are merely means, and others are ends in themselves). We come to see that the goods we aim at most of the time do not add up to much, that they are trivial, or that they are good for leading to destinations that we seldom seem to reach. These are the common frustrations of any human life that admits the least amount of reflection. We are not just biological beings; we are reflective intentional beings. And it is natural for such beings to form second-order desires. We want something more than the satisfaction of trivial wants or wants for mere means. We want the whole activity, the unstopping succession of desire and fulfilment, to be itself aiming at something, and something that is not trivial and not a mere means. That is, I think, the characteristic aim of a reflective intentional being. It is characteristic despite the fact that it is not especially common. What is uncommon is forming the desire in any explicit way. But it takes just a whiff of our own mortality for just about any of us to wonder whether we have had a good life, or whether we have wasted our life. When prompted, every normal reflective agent— the philosopher in the study or the person in the street—asks the question, and hopes to be able to give a certain answer. Bertrand Russell, at the age of 95, started a summing-up of his life in this way: 'The time has come to review my life as a whole, and to ask whether it has served any useful purpose or has been wholly concerned in futility.'[1] These large-scale, course-of-life desires emerge with the move from a merely biological being to a reflective intentional one. Human nature is both biological and intentional; all these interests are part of *human* nature. These course-of-life desires open a space for a certain range of prudential values. Russell went on to write that he could not yet decide whether his life had been futile; it would all depend upon whether his work to lessen the chance of nuclear war had had much success. Certainly lessening the risk of nuclear war is the kind of achievement that would save a life from futility. And that is virtually the definition of the prudential value 'accomplishment': the achievement of the kind of value that gives life weight or point.

Suppose, then, that I am right in thinking that non-biological interests, such as accomplishment and deep personal relations, are as firmly embedded in human nature as biological ones are. To put it roughly, biological ones are embedded in our animal nature, and non-biological ones in our rational nature. This shift from biological to intentional beings is related to the sort of movement that in the last chapter I called explanation by ascent. The shift allows us to explain certain things that we could not explain before. We take a biological being that happens, unlike most other biological beings, to be capable of intentionality, and in effect create a new kind of being by turning what was before merely an accidental property, intentionality, into an essential one.[2] I asked in the last chapter whether this represented a move from natural science to metaphysics. Whatever the word 'metaphysics' might imply in this context, it should not be taken to imply that this sort of shift does not go on within the natural sciences as well. We take certain molecular structures that happen, unlike most others, to be alive, and, by turning life into an essential property, create a new being, a cell. If this act of creation is metaphysics, then metaphysics need not lie outside the natural sciences.

Still, the shift from biological to non-biological interests brings with it other shifts that we cannot ignore: for instance, a shift from predominantly experiential sorts of harm such as pain and ailment, which are fairly easily identified, to non-experiential sorts of harm. What concerns us now is the *reliability* of prudential judgements. How do I know that lack of food is harmful? Well, physical symptoms appear. How do I know that lack of accomplishment is harmful? Well, because life is empty in a certain way—namely (and here circularity threatens), it lacks accomplishment. The way I know that you are less well off if you accomplish nothing in your life is by my having the right value-concept—namely, 'accomplishment'—and so my knowing that it is a value-concept. How do I know that? Are there criteria for those non-experiential sorts of harm that would allow judgements about them to be correct or incorrect?

We cannot identify something as an instance of the value 'accomplishment' by recognizing entirely response-free natural properties; the simple reductive naturalist model, I suggested in the last chapter, fails. Nor can we identify it by recognizing a set of such properties and then by reacting to them with approval, as the Humean model has it. Nor can its identification be by some mode of direct perception of a value realm, as some forms of the intuitionist model have it. This intuitionist model reduces complex judgements about harm to analogy with uncomplicated cases of perception; it would be equally implausible to regard 'dangerous' as the name of yet another object in the realm of values, rather than as something we learn by understanding interactions between the external world and vulnerable humans.

The only plausible account of how we identify prudential values is, I think, more complex than any of these models. The plausible account, I suggested in the last chapter, gives a role to both recognition and reaction, but without the sharp separation of the two that the Humean model makes central. Reaction is nothing as simple as a sentiment of approval; certain standards of appropriateness are essential to its being the reaction that it is. And recognition is not itself fully describable without appeal to reactive elements. It is not that the recognitional and reactive components are there in this complex mix as separable, still independent parts. That separation itself is what seems impossible to maintain. Desire is not blind; reason is not inert. Philosophers did a service in distinguishing between recognition and reaction, but a disservice in separating them so sharply.

So the notion of recognition is best understood as something not entirely reaction-free (and vice versa). Recognition involves, somewhere in its operation, a characteristic human sense of importance. 'Accomplishment' is achieving the sort of thing that, to put it briefly, fulfils life. Being 'fulfilled', in the sense needed, is not a matter of having a feeling of fulfilment; it is a matter of life's not being empty or futile or wasted. Of course, a notion such as 'wasted' is itself evaluative, so a value is already built into our notion of 'life-fulfilling', a value that manifests itself in not just any object's being a possible object of fulfilment. What goes on in recognizing that something is life-fulfilling needs to be described using concepts that, unlike the terms 'reason' and 'desire' after Hume had finished moulding them into terms of art, avoid the active/passive split. The active/passive split has such a strong grip on us, I suspect, because it is a reflection of the mind/body split that has so strongly gripped—and distorted—understanding, not just in philosophy, but in the popular imagination as well. The Cartesian picture of the mind does not make it totally passive, but it limits its activity to what is necessary for various forms of cognition—for example, of connections between ideas, of the clarity and distinctness of ideas. The body, by contrast, has to do with motion in extended space, so that such mental phenomena, in the everyday sense of the term, as appetite, perception, and desire all figure on the physical side of the great divide. Most of us now accept that this picture has to be given up, that we need concepts that occupy the middle ground. So we do with values; and 'recognition' and 'reaction' on the impure, inseparably mixed interpretations that I am suggesting, are meant to be some.

'Recognition', in this impure sense, is meant to be a kind of sensitivity to something in the world. But one is not entitled to talk in terms of sensitivity unless one can explain what it is for the sensitivity to work well and what to work badly. We have a clear, well-established account of the physical senses' working. A theory of what goes on in the world includes an explanation of what goes on in perception. We rely on our perceptions to justify the theory, and the theory to justify our reliance on our perceptions. But the theory explains, among other things, why perceptions in certain conditions are as a body reliable, how they fail, and how we can sometimes detect and correct their failure. Is anything approaching this possible for value judgements? If not, why think that what we have got is a sensitivity *to* anything in the world?

Now, one might see hopes of developing an error theory for *moral* judgements, if one thought (as I do) that they are grounded in some way in (largely human) interests. Moral judgements go wrong, one could say, if they fail to retain certain sorts of links with interests. But we are concerned now not with moral judgements but with judgements about interests themselves, and they seem to be, as far as value judgements go, ground-floor. In their case, we must fall back on our understanding of what goes on in prudential deliberation. But our aims in prudential deliberation are not radically different from our aims in understanding our physical environment. In the latter case, we want to understand what objects confront us in the surroundings in which we must survive and their causal interactions (especially with us), in order that we may find our way around in the world better. In the former case, we want to understand what is present in our human environment when we arrive by a process of explanation by ascent at the level of human interests. To do that, we shall need to make a taxonomy of the domain of human interests (something like my profile of prudential values), just as we have needed to make one of the domain of plants and animals. Human interests are prominent in both projects, and if they have extra prominence in the second one, that is for the unsurprising reason that they are, after all, its subject.

Though operating at ground-floor level, the sensitivity is complex in its workings and fairly rich in its connections. We can say a fair amount about what is needed for it to work well. One has to have a lot of knowledge of the familiar, undisputed factual sort about the world. One has to have sufficient human capacities to know how enjoyment, say, figures in human life. In this way, one can build up an account of the conditions for the successful working of sensitivity to prudential value, akin to conditions such as good light, good eyes, and good position for successful seeing. The account of failure in the sensitivity is independent of most judgements that the sensitivity should deliver. To show that it failed, one must be able to show that the person concerned lacked the concept, or information, or certain human capacities, and the test for lacking any of them is fairly well removed from the deliverance of the sensitivity. For instance, to show that I lack certain human capacities for feeling, you would have to go to empirical psychology or, more rarely, to genetics to show how the difference from a normal human psyche came about. One ought to be able to build up an account of the conditions in which, if all are met, the sensitivity *succeeds*. If so, this sensitivity will differ from a sensitivity such as sight, not in there being no account of its working, but in the greater difficulty of knowing when the conditions for its working are met.[3]

Is that the trouble then—that we never get adequate evidence that they are all met? A full account of prudential deliberation suggests to me that in the right conditions we are sensitive to certain things' making life go better. There are, of course, other explanations of what is going on besides the existence of such a sensitivity, but there are examples that make them seem implausible. For instance, we aim at some things simply because of deep, largely invisible social pressures. But there are also persons who come up with new (to them, at least) value notions, such as accomplishment, that have never been taught to them and the ethos of whose society is live-for-the-moment. In the end, the best explanation of such changes is that the person has hit on, has become sensitive to, something valuable, and that its being valuable is to some extent independent of the process of coming to regard it as such. A sensitivity to values would also be a good explanation of convergence of belief between persons, especially if the convergence emerged when the conditions of reliability were present but most else—social ethos, psychological bent, economic class—were very different. One could hope for simpler, more direct evidence, but this evidence is neither out of reach nor negligible.

3. *Are prudential values real?*

Judgements about prudential values can be correct or incorrect. But that is a fairly weak conclusion, and it can be strengthened. They are correct not just in their use of language, but also as judgements. And they are correct as judgements not in Kant's sense of being required simply by reason, independent of any individual person's attitudes or goals. Although objectivity, in Kant's sense, provides correct value judgements, it does not provide ones that can be considered true, or matters of knowledge, in senses of those terms that we do not want to lose. But judgements about prudential values at any rate—moral values are another question altogether—look like a matter of truth and knowledge in those senses. They seem to be reporting the deliverances of a sensitivity to certain things going on in the world: namely, interests being met or not met. These interests are part of *human* nature, and not just human nature as seen by one society. As biological beings, we have an interest in nourishment; without it we ail. As rational beings, we have an interest in accomplishment; without it life is empty in certain ways. The notion of 'meeting an interest' is rather like the notion 'soothes': something is relieved. We think of both 'soothes' and 'meets an interest' as being, to put it in rough, intuitive language, not properties *in* objects but properties *of* objects, properties relating to the objects' powers of interaction with other things.[4] There is a rich causal base for a judgement about 'soothes'. But judgements about 'soothes' cannot be reduced to a causal base of purely chemical and physiological happenings, because what has to be explained is how certain chemical and physiological processes manifest themselves in human feelings, reference to which is indispensable. The two properties are certainly different, but one should not exaggerate the difference. And their similarity raises the question: Is the property of meeting an interest, like the property of being soothing, out there in the real world? Are prudential values real?

The question of the realism of values is of such deep obscurity that, more than is standard in philosophy, we are groping as much toward a question as toward an answer. In any case, what does it matter, or, at any rate, matter to me now with my present interests, whether prudential values are real? Values are puzzling; they are far from obviously part of the natural world, yet there is no other world obviously available to house them. So we can raise the question about realism in a purely speculative, metaphysical spirit, wanting to understand how values fit into the scheme of things. But we can also raise it, as I do now, for more practical purposes. What matters to us all, and certainly to me now, is the reliability of our ethical beliefs. Realism matters to that; it matters to our need to understand what sort of standards are available for ethical judgement, and what sort of authority our meeting those standards delivers. It is not enough to say that ethical judgements can be not only correct but also true, because 'true' is such an elastic term that it can be properly used by a mathematician about the equation $7 + 5 = 12$ without commitment to realism about numbers, simply because that equation qualifies as a claim with standards of warranted assertibility that have in this case been met; or perhaps even by a philosopher who regards value judgements merely as expressions of the judger's attitude.[5] If we want some enlightenment about the authority our ethical beliefs might have, we must be able to say somewhat more about the kind of truth they have—for instance, whether they might be true in a sense that includes some element of correspondence with a belief-independent reality. We want confidence without complacency— in short, reliability. And we want a higher-order reliability: a reliability in our belief that certain of our first-order ethical beliefs really can be counted on. So we need to encroach at least a bit on the fairly large territory covered by realism.

The strong, simple, intuitive idea behind realism is that there is a lot that exists independently of human perception and judgement, that such things would exist even if no perception and judgement ever took place, and that it is the job of perception and judgement to register and comprehend them, to the extent that they can. This simple, intuitive form of realism fits most comfortably a certain, once seriously entertained, now rejected, conception of the mind and its place in nature. On this conception, things and events make 'impressions' upon the senses or upon the internal sense of introspection, the mind being a device that registers them largely passively. Language is then seen as a matter of attaching labels to these representatives of things or to the things themselves.

This picture now rightly strikes us as naïve. There is no pure given, independent of human interpretation and belief. As most of us agree about that, yet want, none the less, to retain some sort of distinction between realism and irrealism, we have to detach it from this naïve conception of language and knowledge. It goes without saying that we should have no access to a belief-independent reality except through our beliefs. All the same, a belief-independent reality may play a role in explaining at least some of the language in which our beliefs are expressed, some of the beliefs we have, how we justify certain beliefs, how various of us arrive in certain circumstances at the same belief, and (though this just summarizes the points about meaning and justification) in what the truth of certain beliefs consists.[6]

That rough conception of realism, then, suggests an equally rough test for something's being real. We see a belief-independent reality as playing a role in affecting our concepts, our beliefs, our sometimes converging on the same belief. We attribute reality to some kind of thing—any kind at all, including values—in assigning a certain sort of explanatory role to it. One sort of explanatory role that would seem to have these existential implications—sufficient for them, but perhaps not necessary—is causal. This gives us a test of realism in terms of the best causal explanation: realism about a kind of thing is the view that things of that kind must appear in the best account of what happens in the world. The test is quite general; it is not confined to causation in which humans as experiencers or perceivers are involved. If entities such as electrons must appear in the best account of what happens in the world, then there *are* electrons; if properties such as electrical charges appear in the best account of what happens in the world, then there *are* electrical charges. But we are interested in prudential values, and they are unlikely to interact with things other than persons (and animals).

The causal test has its troubles.[7] At first sight, it looks as if it represents an objectionable reductionism.[8] Causation occurs in the natural domain, so the test may seem to assume the reduction of values to facts. But this suspicion of reductionism ignores the possibility of expansive naturalism; perhaps values are, without reduction, also part of the natural world. Or if the point is that causation occurs only in some fairly narrowly defined natural domain (say, as Hume would define it), then it amounts to saying that values, unreduced, are not the sort of thing that can enter causal relations.[9] That has indeed been said. Some philosophers have doubted, on grounds familiar since Hume, whether desires and beliefs are the sorts of thing that can be causes. And if they cannot, then intentions, interests, and values are unlikely to be able to be so either. Hume's idea is that causal connections must be established empirically; they cannot be supplied by meanings. It must be an open question whether if the red billiard-ball hits the stationary white ball, the white one moves. As we cannot identify a desire or an intention independently of its object, the relation between a desire to sing 'Dixie' and one's singing 'Dixie' may be of the wrong kind for causation. But this demand for logical independence between cause and effect is too strong. Not even Hume's paradigm case of one billiard-ball's colliding with another meets it. The statements 'The red collided with the white' and 'The white rolled away' are not logically independent. One could not identify the red and the white in the first place as balls, as physical objects, without presupposing certain facts about how they interact.

Perhaps the most troublesome feature of the causal test is that it depends upon the identification of a 'best' explanation, and our criteria for 'best' can, when hard pressed, become very rough and intuitive. I mentioned this in the last chapter. We resort to some such thing as the causal test because of the inadequacy of our intuitions about what is real; but if sometimes in choosing the 'best' causal explanation, our intuitions about what is real are at work, we are not much further forward. At worst, the argument becomes circular: for some reason we are satisfied that values, say, are real, so what seems to us the best explanation of our value belief, or the convergence of several people's value beliefs, is that there is a value causing it. How much of a threat such circularity poses will vary from case to case.

Despite these imperfections, the causal test seems to me the best available. It may be too strong—sufficient, but not necessary. But I fall back on it for two reasons: I cannot myself find a satisfactory weaker one,[10] and there seems to me to be a case for saying that many prudential values (moral properties or standards are not now in question) pass it.

Do prudential values—not someone's valuing something or other, but simply those values—appear in the best explanation of why some people are in some of the states they are? The typical judgement about prudential values takes the form '*That* meets *this* interest'. For instance, 'That ointment soothes this irritation'; 'That drink slakes her thirst'; 'That accomplishment makes my life fulfilled'. Prudential values are what meet basic human interests. So a prudential value such as accomplishment enters into an explanation of why people are in certain respects as they are—namely, with interests met or unmet. It explains why some people suffer from a sense of emptiness or futility, especially at the end of life, whereas others do not. The value can be at work on us even without our being conscious of it, even, indeed, without our having the concept of 'accomplishment'. The absence of the value can explain the vague, unfocused dissatisfaction with life that can come before we can explain it.

Irrealists about values will not be impressed by this line of thought. One does not have to cite a *value*, they are likely to reply, to explain this sense of emptiness; all that one needs to cite is a *belief* that one's life is empty, and all that one needs to cite to explain the vague, unfocused sense of emptiness is a vague, unfocused belief. But this reply falls short at two points. First, it goes no way toward explaining why the emptiness in question seems to occupy much the same sort of place in our life as an irritation that some ointment might soothe; both are lacks that are part of human nature. It also ignores where the belief that one's life is empty itself comes from. The best explanation of why so many people form the deathbed belief that their life is empty may well be that there is a characteristic human interest often unmet.

So let us shift our attention from human states of being in general to states of belief in particular. I suggested in the previous section that it seemed best to talk in terms of a sensitivity to values in which recognition and reaction are merged. The explanation that I gave of the standards for the successful working of this sensitivity was, ultimately, an account of how values interact with people. We recognize a lack, an interest; furthermore, we recognize that certain things fill the lack or meet the interest. That is, we recognize a value by recognizing certain things that characteristically go on in human life. The best explanation of certain people's belief that something or other is prudentially valuable is that there are features of human life that they recognize. The best explanation of, say, someone's coming up with a new (to them) value notion, such as accomplishment, is that the person has become sensitive in this way to a value, to a capacity that something or other has to meet an interest.

Then there is the phenomenon of convergence of belief between several persons. Most facts about convergence and divergence in normative beliefs are irrelevant to the causal test. There can be complete convergence, and realism none the less be false. There can be great divergence, and realism still be true. There can even be little prospect of convergence among all rational persons, or among all humans, and realism still be true; convergence on some matter of value could well be limited to persons of a certain culture who have brought off the rare feat of developing the conceptual apparatus that allows them to think about these subjects.[11] What matters to the causal test is what explains the convergence or divergence. That is a particularly tangled empirical issue. But if, when certain knowledge and sensitivity and conceptual equipment are all in place, convergence in belief occurs, and if that happens when other causal influences on the formation of belief, such as social pressures, are different, then the best explanation may well turn out to be the workings of the recognition that I was just talking about. Certainly, if the explanation I suggested in the one-person case is plausible, it will be a likely candidate in the many-person case.

Would these results, if indeed they were forthcoming, be worth calling 'realism'? Well, the property 'life-fulfilling' seems to be a feature of things in the world in much the way that the property 'soothing' is. But that may not yet take us to realism, and there is an altogether more radical thought that threatens to block the way. Accomplishment is a prudential value only because we regard a life without it as wasted. The notion 'life-fulfilling' is parasitic upon the negative notion 'life-wasting'. The notion 'wasted' is evaluative; among other things, it gives expression to a natural human desire. Yet, that does not serve to distinguish it from the property 'soothing'. The notion 'soothing' is parasitic upon the notion 'irritation', and 'irritation', like all members of the extended 'pain' family, has among the criteria for its use what humans characteristically want to avoid or have alleviated. Much of language—Wittgenstein seems to suggest all of it—has meaning only within the context of natural human concerns and desires, interests, sense of importance, and so on. This raises the possibility that the embeddedness of our concepts in the human point of view is so deep that it makes no sense to speak of a belief-independent reality. Is there a case for a wide irrealism that would carry a narrower irrealism about values along with it?

This is the point at which I can disengage from the issues of realism. Without doubt, much of language is possible only within the human perspective, and therefore much of what we believe to be true is relative to that perspective, though this is not relativism in any familiar sense of the term; nor is it necessarily threatening to any of the things that relativism in the familiar sense is. I disengage because I have got what I want from this incursion into realism: namely, a somewhat fuller understanding of the way in which judgements about prudential values can be true.

A judgement about something's being 'life-fulfilling' can be true in the way that judgements about 'soothing' can be. Both are judgements about what goes on in the world of (human) nature. They are true in virtue of that bit of the natural world. The fact that the concepts 'soothing' and 'life-fulfilling' are deeply embedded in the human perspective, the fact that recognizing their occurrence necessarily involves a human response, does not undermine their truth. The response goes into making something 'soothing' or 'life-fulfilling', rather than being a truth-undermining part of the criteria for judging it actually to be soothing or life-fulfilling. And nature consists of objects, properties, and events that are independent of our ideas and beliefs about them, in the following sense. Our ideas are shaped by what they are ideas of; we can alter an idea, or even drop some ideas and invent new ones, as we discover more about nature or just reflect more deeply on what we already know. And we confirm our beliefs against nature—that is the truistic version of the correspondence theory of truth. We look more closely; we collect evidence; we find counter-examples.

These are the ordinary ways in which we establish the truth of a claim that a certain ointment soothes a certain irritation. Such judgements are about matters of fact, and if the evidence is good enough, they can be especially reliable. What is important to me here is whether judgements about prudential values can be too.

4. Expanding the list of especially reliable beliefs

May we, then, add some prudential judgements to the list of especially reliable beliefs? Not simply because prudential values are (at least in the modest sense that I have just sketched) real. Realism sometimes positively invites scepticism—for instance, when the belief-independence that realism incorporates puts reality so far into the background that the human mind has trouble making contact with it. But that something affects one's life for better or worse cannot be out of touch with our belief. Nothing could be in a particular person's interest that fell outside human awareness in general. For example, something's being life-fulfilling in the way that an accomplishment is cannot be outside the range of human sensitivity. I might be unaware of something that I had accomplished (say, because the evidence that I had actually succeeded— as in Russell's case with reducing the risk of nuclear war—might not fully surface until after I die), but, despite this, it might still count as making my life prudentially better.[12] That, however, is a different point: what is outside one's awareness in this case is one particular piece of evidence, not all evidence of that kind.

Nor can we add prudential judgements to the list just because they are the working of a sensitivity with standards of correctness. Reports of a sensitivity—say, sight—are not, as such, especially reliable; their reliability depends upon such things as the state of our eyes, our position, the light, and so on.

None the less, there are reasonable prospects of our being able to add some judgements about non-core prudential values to the list of especially reliable beliefs. Prudential values are deeply embedded in human nature; they are real happenings in a part of our lives accessible to our observation.

I speak merely of reasonable prospects, rather than of solidly bankable assets, because we have not got far with the necessary work. After the Greek and Roman periods, philosophers largely turned away from studying the nature of the good life. In the Jewish-Christian period that followed in Europe, attention was focused on obligations imposed upon people trying to live good lives. In our time, we have first to re-focus attention on the good life; we have then to reflect on how sound our judgements about it are. We must each individually form some views about the profile of prudential values by the sort of deliberation that I talked about in Chapter II. We must explain ourselves to, and ask for explanations from, others, especially others with very different views from our own. Then we must hope for convergence, which, especially if it happens in the right circumstances, will increase our confidence that the shared sensitivity that we think is at work is actually at work.

How much, then, can we add to the list of especially reliable beliefs? The project that I just recommended is not far enough advanced for us to say. And we have not even begun considering moral standards. So we do not yet know, either, how far this larger list of especially reliable beliefs will take us in assessing competing moral views. Let me turn now to moral standards, in order to fill that gap.

V

A SIMPLE MORAL THOUGHT

1. *A glance back*

We are looking for especially reliable ethical beliefs. We should not assume that all ethical beliefs, as a kind, have the same epistemological standing. My guess is that, on the contrary, prudential beliefs differ from moral ones, and that moral beliefs are not uniform among themselves either. That is why, in the last chapter, I discussed prudential beliefs separately. I arrived at what I thought could be counted as—in a fairly loose sense of the term—a realist view of prudential values and a connected view about our knowledge of them. And now I want, for the same reason, to discuss different kinds of moral beliefs separately. Some moral standards seem to me not to go far beyond the prudential values to which they are related, and so to borrow a lot of the standing of those values, while others get very much further away from prudential values, and, accordingly, need quite different things said of them.

2. *The line between prudence and morality*

My approach seems to assume a sharp line between prudence and morality. But the line, I think, is not sharp. We can neither understand morality independently of prudence, nor live well prudentially independently of living well morally.

Some moral standards, I suggest, are just a short step from prudential values. And the view of prudential values that I proposed earlier is this. My seeing something as prudentially good for me requires my seeing it as good for persons generally. It is not that certain specific things, such as an empty box of matches to complete my collection, cannot be valuable to me and not generally. But if anything is valuable, it is because it fits under some heading or other of things valuable to persons generally: such headings as freedom from pain, enjoyment, accomplishment, and so on. My merely desiring something, even intensely, cannot itself turn it into a value. And value headings name things that are generally or typically valuable, not necessarily universally so. Something valuable typically may turn out not to be valuable to an atypical person.

Some prudential values enter the very conception of a human being. We see each other as humans, and understand what each says and does, only because we accept that we have many beliefs and concerns in common.[1] For me to see you as human is to see you as having certain physical and psychological states that you want to avoid or to have alleviated, as having goals that can be achieved or frustrated, as finding certain things enjoyable or important, and so on.

One can go further. Prudence, I suspect, involves not only recognizing that values are at stake in other persons' lives, but also to some degree, yet to be made clear, respecting the values at stake in other lives. I have already said that one cannot make a clean cut between prudence and morality. That, I think, is an understatement. Each, in fact, infiltrates the other deeply, in the following ways.

There are several, irreducibly different prudential values: enjoyment, accomplishment, certain kinds of understanding, the elements of human dignity (autonomy, liberty, minimum material provision), and so on. The more one tries to explain these prudential values, the more one finds a huge hole in them that has to be filled by the value represented by other persons. All I can offer now are more speculations than arguments, because successful arguments depend upon the correct identification of prudential values, and prudential value theory is underdeveloped, even by the undemanding standards of the rest of ethics. What is not speculative, though, is that how independent prudence and morality are of one another turns, in part, upon the nature (sometimes upon the fine texture) of prudential values.

For example, one prudential value is deep personal relations. One's 'deep personal relations', in the technical sense that the term takes on when it names a prudential value, are relations that contribute to making one's life fulfilled. That contribution is necessary to a relation's being of the right sort; it imposes a constraint on the kinds of personal relations that will count. They would have to be relations of love and friendship. One person would have to care greatly about the other, recognize and want to promote the other's good. To speak of these personal relations as making one's own life fulfilled makes it sound as if their value is entirely self-centred; but this example illustrates instead an old piece of wisdom that some self-centred values require a large measure of other-centring. Some people will no doubt think that all I am speaking of here is natural affection, and that natural affection is not yet morality. I am suspicious of the conceptions of morality that are likely to be behind such a remark, with their own sharp line between natural affection and ethics; but I shall not press the issue, but propose only this. One cannot describe this prudential value fully without bringing in our recognition of, and response to, the value represented by (some) other persons.

Another value is accomplishment. The sorts of successes that one can count as 'accomplishment', in my technical sense, are ones that give a life point or substance. Again, this result is necessary for a success to be of the right sort. Counting blades of grass in various lawns, unusual and difficult an achievement as it no doubt is, would not rate; whereas increasing people's understanding of important matters or finding a cure for a major illness would—in general, doing something that substantially benefited others would rate. Perhaps there are accomplishments whose weighty value does not come from benefiting others. Solving some puzzle in pure mathematics might be an example. Still, the more one doubted that the solution met any substantial human interest, the more one would suspect that it failed to give any life much point or weight. In any case, one would have no grasp of the very largest class of accomplishments that human life affords if one did not introduce the value represented by other persons. Most accomplishments, and the sorts of accomplishments accessible to most of us, involve benefits to others.

Take one more example. Not any piece of knowledge counts as 'understanding' when that word is used to mark a prudential value. Some knowledge is trivial, some simply the wrong kind. What seems to me to count as 'understanding' in this technical sense concerns, to put it roughly, one's place in the scheme of things. It includes certain metaphysical and moral matters, such as whether there is a God, the value of life, the value represented by other persons. It includes the sort of understanding that would be part of Socrates' ideal of an 'examined life'. And what is valuable is an examined *life*. The prudential value of understanding is not exhausted by a detached, passive contemplation of these values; it also includes coming to terms with them. A life in which one not only perceives those values, but also responds appropriately to them, is better, simply in prudential terms, than one in which one only perceives them. And this residual value is not, I think, caught by any of the other prudential value-terms, although 'accomplishment' starts to overlap with 'understanding' at a certain point. Part of this prudential value involves accommodating certain moral values.

3. *Egoism and altruism*

We date the start of 'modern' philosophy from Descartes. He wanted to turn our ramshackle common-sense beliefs into a solid structure. In search of firm foundations, he retreated from beliefs about an external world, which he found shaky, back to beliefs about our own private, internal experiences. But once we retreat inside our own minds, can we find any rational route out? I myself am sympathetic to the view that it is not possible intelligibly to retreat to a world of one's own private experiences. One cannot get inside, so there is no problem about how to get out.

There is a parallel, though less neat, story to be told about 'modern' moral philosophy, with Hobbes playing Descartes's role. Altruistic reasons for action are psychologically suspect, and therefore, for theory-building purposes, shaky. But self-interested reasons (in Hobbes's case, a quite specific one: to save one's own skin) are beyond doubt; they are part of our biological nature. Take self-interested rationality, therefore, as primary, and altruism as derivative. Practical rationality, on this model, starts with self-interest, and works outwards from it.

The parallel is not perfect: there were more resisters to the retreat into self-interest than there were to the retreat into private experience. Still, in one form or another, the tradition of the primacy of self-interest has been strong in philosophy, and dominant in the social sciences. In a theoretical framework like that, certain questions become pressing and difficult: How do we get to mutually beneficial co-operation? Once we retreat inside self-interest, is there any rational route out? And there is a parallel answer. The considerations in the last section go some way toward suggesting that it is very hard to retreat into self-interest. If one cannot get in, the problem is not about getting out. I am sympathetic to that view too.

I am sympathetic for reasons I have touched on briefly before. Pains have both a phenomenological side to them (the internal feel of our experiences) and, equally important, an active side (reactions and responses of avoidance, alleviation, and so on). One learns the word 'pain' both by having certain experiences and by understanding where pains fit into human life—that 'pains' are to be avoided or alleviated. This reactive element is not sharply separable from the recognitional element. And this is so not because, with pain, recognitional elements and reactive elements, though separable in principle, are difficult to disentangle, but because the distinction between these two kinds of elements ceases to hold here. And that is because our standard of sameness in the sensations that we group together under the concept 'pain' is partly that they are what are to be avoided, alleviated, and so on. With pains, we do not recognize something to which we also, independently, react. Our reaction is a constituent of our recognition. The way pain fits into human life is part of the criterion for its being pain.[2] Therefore, my knowing that you are in pain involves my knowing something that is a disvalue to you. The distinction between fact and value, as one finds it in Hume and in most moral philosophy in the analytic tradition, becomes difficult at this point to sustain. My judgement that you are in pain looks factual, but it is also, inescapably, a judgement about a disvalue.

My seeing myself as a person is seeing myself as a chooser. My agency is manifested in a stream of intentional actions. Sometimes, as with reflex actions or involuntary starts, I simply observe myself moving. But normally when I act, I both have an aim and have beliefs about how to bring it about, so I am not reduced to the role of an observer with regard to my own actions. Occasionally our desires come as unwelcome afflictions—for instance, the compulsion to wash one's hands yet again. But the desires at the heart of our conception of agency are different in kind from these: our practical thought and our intentional action aim at meeting interests or avoiding their frustration, and they are faulty on their own terms if they fail. My sense of my interests is central to my sense of being an agent and a person living a life. My sense of your being an agent and a person living a life involves my attributing interests to you. It involves, even, my attributing to you at least some of my own basic interests.

So, my sense of you as a human being brings along with it my acceptance that you are guided through life by many of the same interests that are guiding me, and that those interests play the same role in your life as they do in mine. There are values at stake in my life; there are values, many of them the same, at stake in yours. There cannot be values at stake in my life unless there are also values at stake in yours, and some must be the same. What I shall, or should, do about you is still an open question. What I *shall* do depends upon the state of my motivation, and what I *should* do depends upon moral norms for action, which we have not broached yet. But what is no longer in question is this measure of agreement in values between us.

Now motivation is internal to something's being a general human interest. That follows from the earlier rejection of any sharp split in these cases between recognition and reaction. My recognizing pain as a disvalue cannot be detached from the characteristic human response to it. A characteristic response, of course, need not be a universal one; for instance, people can get so deeply depressed that the natural human dynamics of that recognition shut down.[3]

It is, I think, a fairly small, but not entirely straight, step from *general human interest* to *reason for action*. If something is such an interest, then it is capable of generating a reason for action. The step is not entirely straight because I think that we must recognize other reason-generating considerations. My having an interest in avoiding pain gives me a reason to avoid it. What pain is in my life is normally the same as what it is in yours. So I think that your having the same interest in avoiding pain also works as a reason-generating consideration for me. But other reason-generating considerations may also have to be present—the benefit to you, let us say, is great and the cost to me negligible (I just have to dial 999)—before I have a reason to relieve your pain. I shall return in a moment to the conception of practical reason that I have just begun to sketch here.

That, of course, is an infamous, much scrutinized move in

philosophy—from my pain's giving me a reason for action to your pain's also (potentially) giving me a reason. The step can look daunting if we see ourselves starting from within purely self-interested reasons, as if they were secure, and then trying to build upon them. If we accept that as our project, then unless we can establish, while standing on the narrow ground of self-interest, an entirely new category of practical reason, we are left with the hard job of reducing non-egoistic to egoistic reasons.

My suggestion is that there is no such step—no step because what works as a reason-generating consideration for me when I am in pain also works for me when you are in pain. The obvious difference between my reason to relieve my pain and my reason to relieve yours is that in one case it is *my* pain and in the other it is *yours*. But the engine of the two judgements, as we understand them, is *pain: because it hurts*. The 'my' and 'your' are not part of the reason-generating consideration. The clause *because it hurts* lacks reference to me or to you, but it lacks nothing of what we take the disvalue to be. To try to deny 'pain' its status as a disvalue or a reason unless it is attached to 'my' would mean giving up our present grasp of how 'pain' works as a reason for action.[4]

Where I find no step, others find a notoriously troublesome one. Of course, if pain itself is bad, then there is no step to take. But why think of the reason like that? Perhaps I am right that I cannot see others as fellow human beings without acknowledging that their pain matters in their lives in just the way that my pain matters in mine. And, true, that forces me to a kind of universalization: everyone's pain gives that person a reason to act. But that is not the universalization: everyone's pain can give everyone a reason to act. Shrewd egoists see good and bad as tied to an individual; pain, they can say, is not bad *simpliciter* but bad for *x*. If egoists accept that it is bad *simpliciter*, then, of course, they cut the ground from under their own feet. But if they do not, they are, it seems, rationally impregnable.[5]

But they are not impregnable. The question merely becomes: Who is right? Is pain bad *simpliciter*, or bad for *x*? And here one cannot, it is true, expect much in the way of argument, because what is in question is the character of a quite basic reason. Still, what one can do is to supply the background for these reasons—for instance, by describing as fully as one can how we decide what is prudentially valuable, what standards are available to us, and what constraints there are on values and reasons. Then one can at least say something stronger than that most of us do in fact see pain as bad *simpliciter*. One can say that, given the best background against which to look at it, this seems the natural way to take it. This, of course, says nothing more than what I have already said: the best account of the reason-generating consideration is *because it hurts*, without reference to the agent to whom the reason is addressed.

Why, then, have so many people found the step so troublesome? There are, no doubt, many reasons, each at best only part of the whole answer. One's conception of well-being plays a role. Classical utilitarians conceived of well-being as a state of consciousness.[6] It is easy then to pose the question, Why should one locus of consciousness care what is happening at another? But if well-being is not a matter just of individual consciousness, if prudential values can involve one person's accommodating the value represented by other persons, then that is not the question one would want to ask.

The main reason, however, is that the sceptics are in an important way right, and for at least two reasons. There is a big, troublesome step to take from self-interest to concern for others—so troublesome, in fact, that it is far from clear that many of us can take it. And, second, anything approaching a full account of pain-based reasons for action will indeed give weight to the 'my' or 'your'; egoism is in that respect right; it is only that the relevant weight seems to me to tip the balance away from complete impartiality rather than toward egoism.

There *is* a big and troublesome step. The enormous problem is how we move human agents, who are genetically programmed to be highly selfish and whose natural concern for others is limited and fragile, to act better. The problem is that we are programmed in a primitive form of egoism; we care about only a small range of prudential values: our own survival, advancement, and gratification, and that of a few others. There is also the educated egoism that I was just talking of, in which one recognizes the full range of prudential values and their penetration by elements of morality. But primitive egoism is where we naturally start; educated egoism is merely where reflection eventually leads a very few of us.[7] It is not much of an advance toward a solution to the vital practical problem of getting us to act better to establish that, whether agents know it or not, they often have a reason to show various forms of respect to others. How do we take the step from your pain's giving me a reason to act to its giving me a reason of sufficient, effective strength actually sometimes to overcome my own insistent primitive self-interest? To solve that problem, we need to put before people's minds considerations that will sometimes, without coercion, get them listening to their self-concern less and to their concern for others more. And that is, in a way, a matter of giving them reasons—not getting them to see that *because it hurts* can give them some reason to be concerned for others, but giving them reasons to see themselves and others, and to see what constitutes success in life, in such a way that they will be more prepared than they are naturally to give others their due. That usually takes a lifetime of training, and success is always in doubt.

Success, I think, turns crucially on two things. How much change in human motivation is possible? And how much is needed? Will supply meet demand? One way to tip the natural balance of concern a little more toward others is, paradoxically, to concentrate on what makes one's own life go well. Prudence, one discovers, cannot be kept separate from morality. How would I act if I wanted to promote solely my own interests as much as possible? I should have deep loving relations; I should hope to accomplish things. But this, as I have said, is life without sharp division between concern for self and concern for others. And one has to abandon self-interested motivation too: in a loving relationship one is moved by the other person's good, not by the ultimate pay-off for oneself. I cannot even, in a classically self-interested way, accept these facts and therefore abandon self-interested rationality and motivation, all for a good, self-interested reason and from good, self-interested motivation. That tactic does not take the true measure of the infiltration of prudence by morality. Accomplishment is doing something that matters with one's life, and much that matters does so because of the value that others represent. And we want to understand and respond to reality, including the reality of others. The strategy here is not the philosopher's common one of reducing morality to self-interest; it is the strategy of chipping away at the difference between them. This is one course that moral growth sometimes follows, and there are others.

So change is possible. But how much is demanded? One source

of lively resistance to the move toward total impartiality is the daunting, even slightly repellent, destination. Who could reach it? Who would even want to? To give everyone in the world equal weight to oneself and one's family is, I think, beyond normal human agents. This is a complicated issue, a difficult mix of the empirical and the normative, on which I shall say more in Chapter VI; but I think that the facts go against our being able to be completely impartial. In some sense, 'ought' implies 'can', so perhaps there is no moral reason to be completely impartial. What is more, giving everyone equal weight is not, in any case, the ideal form of human life. One can raise one's capacity for complete impartiality and generalized love of humanity only by reducing one's commitments to particular persons and projects. But a good life is, among other things, a life of accomplishment and deep personal relations, and these demand such commitments. To adopt complete impartiality would be a dreadful denial of human flourishing. And it is no defence that anyone aiming at impartiality, for just that reason, would stop short of abandoning commitments to individuals. To do that would be to abandon the attempt to come as close as one can to giving everyone equal weight.

In abandoning egoism, though, one does not have to go all the way to complete impartiality. Both the limits on practical reasons and the nature of prudential values suggest that there may, after all, be a half-way house. Impartiality is often resisted, I think, because it ignores the limits of the will and the nature of human flourishing. But they can both be acknowledged along with accepting that anyone's pain matters. My accepting that your pain matters, and matters indistinguishably (as far as the badness of the state that you are in) from my pain, is not to accept that your pain weighs (in determining what I should do) as much as my own pain or that of my children. To argue that pains are equally reason-generating considerations, no matter whose they are, is not to argue that pains matter equally in determining what an agent ought to do, no matter whose they are.

This brings me to the second reason why the sceptics are right: the 'my' and the 'your' do have weight in pain-based reasons for action. It is just that it is not the weight that egoists attribute to them. The impersonal consideration *because it hurts*, without completion by *hurts me*, is the universal ground for my pain-based practical reasons. But practical reasons are the product of many considerations. In order to arrive at a full account of pain-based reasons, one has to add to the consideration *because it hurts* certain other considerations that help determine the force and content of those reasons. Whose pain it is also matters, because ours is a life of deep commitments to particular persons and causes; our capacities (our knowledge of the fate of others, certainly, and also our capacity to help) are limited; our responsibilities may be too. It matters whether it is my pain or my child's or a stranger's; it matters how much it would cost me to help. To revert to an earlier point, you might have to be right under my feet and in need of what I can fairly easily provide before the ground consideration *because it hurts*, on its own, gives me a reason to act. And when, on its own, it provides a reason, the full account of that reason will have to bring in the fact that those other considerations with the potential to outweigh or to nullify this ground consideration are in this case absent. This is not egoism: the relevance of *whose* pain it is comes now from such matters as the value of our commitments and our capacities, not from the unique practical weight of *my*. What I am saying now, of course, makes assumptions about what practical reasons are and, in particular, about how considerations about agents can affect an impersonal ground consideration such as *because it hurts*. I shall be coming back to these matters in the next two chapters.

What has begun to emerge from this section and the last is a picture that much modern moral philosophy, with its sharp opposition of self-interest and morality, does not prepare us for. As one's conception of a good personal life matures, one finds it increasingly hard to keep quite separate one's own flourishing from the flourishing of others. There is no place in this picture for an egocentric agent sure about self-interested reasons but doubtful about other-interested ones. No agent will be in a position to entertain any reasons at all without language, and will not have language without accepting some values of the language community—some prudential ones, certainly, and, it seems, a few basic moral ones as well. And it is part of this picture that morality not only penetrates prudence but is also penetrated by it. There is the obvious point that much moral thought is about promoting or protecting individual well-being. But there is a further point. A person with no self-concern lacks the respect for human life that everyone ought to have. Selflessness—that is, regarding oneself as of no weight morally—is not only psychologically pathological but also morally deficient. Decent behaviour rests above all on good dispositions, and what would be most effective for morality is a disposition that renders one unable to act cruelly or greedily or shabbily without considerable shame, without a strong sense of having betrayed one's own best self.[8] In this picture, prudence and morality merge in what we might call, with precedent, *ethics*. Ethics is about how one ought to live. It is more basic than either prudence or morality, which in this picture appear merely as aspects of ethics, useful for certain purposes to distinguish, so long as the distinction is not pressed far.[9]

4. *An example of a moral standard*

My aim in this chapter is to discuss one kind of moral judgement, a kind of judgement close to prudential judgements. Let me now take an example. 'That's cruel' is a judgement about action, but is well short of directing or commanding action, as 'ought' and 'must' judgements do; so it avoids some of the complications about the limits of the will. All the same, 'That's cruel' already encapsulates a standard for behaviour. And I want to ask, How does this standard arise?

That genetic question is crucial to ethics. Moral philosophers ought to be as puzzled by it as young children are about where babies come from. The answer is largely beyond us at present. It will have to be both factual and normative; the full answer will be drawn from evolutionary biology, anthropology, psychology, decision theory, as well as from the patterns of justification that ethics itself seeks to map. All these strands of the answer are relevant to ethics. My own particular answer (in this chapter and the next two) draws on all of them, but is biased toward the normative: can we discern some structure of thought behind certain moral norms that will, to some extent, both explain why they weigh with us and justify their doing so?[10] Even this partial answer will, I think, have some worthwhile consequences for our thought about ethics.

A person who acts 'cruelly' intends to make another suffer gratuitously—that is, not for some greater good. That intention is both necessary and sufficient. If I do something just to hurt you (say, twist your arm), but, by a fluke, save you greater pain (say, by replacing your dislocated shoulder), what I do is none the less cruel. If I try to help you (say, by replacing your dislocated shoulder), but cause you greater pain (say, by breaking your arm), I am clumsy or oafish, but not cruel. That is why doctors, even if bungling, so long as they are not actually evil, are not cruel. And if I punish you because I think that you deserve it, and you do not, then I may be mistaken or irresponsible, but not cruel. The centrality of the agents' intention explains why the cruel infliction of pain can be more hurtful than the same amount of pain inflicted accidentally or thoughtlessly; if it is done cruelly, the sufferer is also degraded as unworthy of concern, as a mere subject of another's power. For you to judge my act not to be cruel, therefore, you do not yourself have to decide that there is some compensatingly greater good; you just have to decide the matter of fact that I think there is.

But, then, is 'That's cruel' not, after all, a moral judgement, which I presented it as, but a factual one? That is what John Mackie thinks. 'What is the connection', he asks, 'between the natural fact that an action is a piece of deliberate cruelty—say, causing pain just for fun—and the moral fact that it is wrong?'[11] Mackie thinks that Hume's model fits: we delineate an action through the natural description 'cruel', and independently respond to it with disapproval, morality then entering through the disapproval. But the notion of 'cruel', I think, leaves no space for disapproval to be a further, independent stage. To understand 'pain' involves regarding it as a disvalue. One cannot delineate the concept of 'pain' in terms of Humean natural facts, and only then look for a response to it. Part of what delineates 'pain' is that it is responded to in a negative way. You respond to your pain negatively, and its having that standing in your life often gives me a reason to avoid causing you pain, and so to avoid being cruel to you. We saw in the previous chapter that the Humean model did not fit prudential values;[12] it does not fit 'cruelty' either.

5. *Deliberation about such a standard*

I discussed deliberation about prudential values in the second chapter. But I concentrated there on prudential values of some complexity, values that especially demanded deliberation, such as accomplishment. There are also prudential values and disvalues so basic, so centrally embedded in our conceptual framework—pain, for instance—that the idea of deliberation scarcely fits. One cannot make sense of those looming presences in our experience, other people, without understanding how, with their vulnerable bodies and psyches, they fit into the world—not least, their being able to be hurt by it. Deliberation is left no space to get going.

When we move on to moral deliberation, we find much the same thing. Some moral notions, such as 'cruel', being conceptually close to 'pain', inherit much of its obviousness. How would one establish that I had a reason not to be cruel to you? My reason comes partly from inevitable features of our conceptual framework: my seeing you as a person involves my accepting that there are certain basic values at stake in your life, and my seeing them as values produces a reason for me to respect them. Again, deliberation hardly gets going.

The obviousness of the judgement 'That's cruel' comes also from its generally being made well within certain boundaries. It is well within the capacity of the human will not to torture cats for fun; the most ordinary people manage it. And it costs us nothing not to torture cats for fun. The judgement 'That's cruel' generally operates within an area in which the human frame can easily deliver what is needed, so the condemnation built into the word 'cruel' is apt.

The same is true of some 'ought' judgements. One sometimes sees a distinction drawn between moral and non-moral 'oughts', but the same semantics fits both. To say that something 'ought to be' is to say that it is what conforms to some standard, norm, or regularity. If, as we stand on the station platform, I say to you, 'The train ought to be in at 9.30', I can justify my claim by pointing to the timetable: its being in at 9.30 is what would conform to the norm established by the timetable. You, being wiser than I in the ways of British Rail, may know that trains regularly run ten minutes late and may counter, 'It ought to be in at about 9.40', and what justifies your claim is that its arriving then is what would conform to practice. That second example explains what are sometimes called 'probability oughts'. 'It ought to be sunny tomorrow' makes the claim that there is some norm or regularity to which sun tomorrow would conform. 'Moral oughts' are no different. They claim merely that there is a norm in the background to which a certain action would conform.

Suppose I can save your life just by tossing you the lifebelt next to me. Then I ought to. What is at stake for you is enormous; the cost to me is negligible. When that is so, one would lose all grip on the notion of reasons for action if one did not accept that I had a reason to help you now. And the reasons are not confined to here and now; they constitute a re-applicable norm or standard which, however it should in the end be formulated, or whether it is in the end formulable, applies at any rate to cases in which the benefit is huge and the cost trivial. And a norm backs an 'ought'.

Not all moral judgements are so simple. As soon as the cost to me is not negligible, I shall certainly want to know who can claim a sacrifice from me and how great that sacrifice can be. Those questions arise, for instance, once moral norms have fairly broad scope. 'You oughtn't to steal.' Not even to save someone's life? Not even my own child's life? Common-sense morality works with a certain rough sketch of human nature; that sketch plays a large role in determining the demands it makes. Every moral theory must work with one sketch or another. The content of moral demands is inevitably influenced by a conception of the person upon whom the demands are laid: what a good individual life is like, what the demands of social life are, what the human frame can deliver. These are partly questions about values, but partly also empirical questions. Even the relatively simple moral term 'cruel' rests on views about human nature, but the views it rests on are for the most part clear and uncontentious. Once we move to other areas of morality, however, the views become less clear and much more contentious.

6. *Special reliability again*

At the end of the last chapter I said that it was easy to find a few beliefs of special reliability—for instance, the core values that are part of the framework only within which our language is intelligible. Avoidance of pain is in that core. The moral judgement 'That's cruel', I say now, does not go much beyond claims about pain and, importantly, intention. It asserts that an act intentionally causes pain without, in the agent's view, serving a greater good. It has whatever reliability judgements about pain, causes, and intentions have. It is likely that at least some judgements on these matters will be especially reliable. What is more, the property 'cruel', being a combination of pain, causes, and intentions, has whatever meta-physical standing they have—some sort of real standing, I am willing to say, though I do not want to try to defend this view. If anyone disagrees, at least we know the focus of the disagreement: whether intentions, say, or pains have a belief-independent exist-ence. I think, though, that most of those who would dispute my explanation of the special reliability of judgements about cruelty, or the real standing of the property 'cruel', disagree at a different point altogether.

The more likely disagreement is this. 'That's cruel' is a moral judgement. It gives a person about to act cruelly a reason to stop. 'Cruel' has a prescriptive force that, according to the objection, my analysis in terms of intention, cause, and pain fails to capture. One can concede to the objector that 'cruel' indeed carries a prescriptive force if that means simply that it gives a reason for action. The question then becomes, How do we explain its reason-giving status? That explanation, I have suggested, is roughly the same as the one for 'pain'. 'It hurts' can generate a reason for me to avoid the thing myself and also a reason not to visit it on you. The reason-generating force of 'cruel' derives from, and has the same explanation as, the reason-generating force of 'pain'. There is no residual force that needs further, reliability-destroying or realism-undermining explanation. (The other two elements in cruelty, intention and cause, are simply features of any reason for action.)

But what if we shift from the fairly neutral, descriptive mode of 'That's cruel' to the overtly prescriptive mode of 'So you ought not to do it'? Do moral 'oughts' harbour a reliability-destroying force? To say 'You ought not to do it' is, I suggested, to say that there is some norm or standard to which your not doing it would conform. The question then becomes, How do we explain the existence of a norm? If something, say pain, is a disvalue, it can generate a reason for action, say to avoid pain. A reason for action can be written as, is a form of, a norm: for example, 'Avoid pain'. Then the question becomes, Is there anything special about *moral* reasons for action or *moral* norms that endows them with different epistemological or metaphysical implications from, say, prudential reasons or norms? 'Avoid pain', of course, can be either. What makes it a moral norm on occasion is that the interest at stake then is another person's.

Moral philosophy in the analytic tradition has been anxious to bring out the different functions served by indicatives and imperatives, by descriptions and prescriptions. It was right that what we do with the one form of speech is typically very different from what we do with the other. But moral philosophy in this tradition has often exaggerated, I think, the metaethical import of these observations. The function of moral 'ought' statements is typically to guide behaviour. But the moral 'ought' statements on which we are focusing now do so by citing a norm the existence and knowledge of which is indistinguishable from the existence and knowledge of interests, causes, and intentions.

7. A look ahead

How should we go about distinguishing better from worse ethical views? That question first led us to a question in metaethics: Are there value judgements of high reliability? That then led us to a question in normative ethics: What critical resources are actually available to us in our normative thought? This now leads us to questions in psychology, sociology, and evolutionary biology. This progression makes metaethics and normative ethics much less independent of one another, and less independent of the sciences, than we often think. We cannot say anything useful about how reliable moral judgements are unless we know something about what creates and shapes moral norms. And we cannot know that without knowing something about the nature of human agents, because among the important forces shaping norms are such things as human capacities and the demands of social co-operation. Ethics must accept some form of requirement of psychological realism, and nothing can count as a moral norm that fails to meet it. Of course, precisely what it requires is obscure, and would be much contested, though clearly everyone would accept it in some form or other. It might turn out that the requirement is so weak that all the ethical views that we now take seriously will pass it, and that it therefore fails to discriminate between them. I think not, and that is what I shall turn to next.

VI

AGENTS

Prudential values do not show us what to do. Though they are generally worth pursuing, they themselves leave it open when, how, for whom, and to what extent—even whether—we should pursue them. But norms such as 'Don't drink more than 21 units of alcohol a week' or 'Don't be cruel' prohibit action.

Once action is at issue, then the nature of agents is too. Prudential goods, to some degree, determine the content of moral norms, but the capacities of agents and facts about their social life begin to play a central role too. The determinants of norms are complex and heterogeneous.

1. *The good life*

One determinant is the nature of the good life. Prudential deliberation, I suggested in Chapter II, ends up with a list of values, such as enjoyment, understanding, accomplishment, deep personal relations, autonomy, and liberty. A striking feature of many items on the list is their long-term, life-structuring character. In that respect, they are quite unlike the sole value in classical utilitarianism, which, on the dominant interpretation, is a mental state, an experience, and so short-term. To have deep attachments to particular persons is to acquire motives that shape much of one's life and carry on through most of it. To accomplish something with one's life requires dedication to particular activities that typically narrow and absorb one's attention. Many prudential values involve commitments—to particular persons, institutions, causes, and careers. One cannot live a prudentially good life, one cannot fully flourish, without becoming in large measure partial. That partiality then becomes part of one; it is not something that one can psychologically enter into and exit from at will. It involves becoming a certain kind of person. Even short-term pleasures have finally to be judged in a fairly long-term, character-fixing way, because a person has to decide how much place to give to living for day-to-day pleasures seen up against competing ways of life.

On the prudential theory that I am proposing, one should become deeply partial. That partiality is, I think, bound to be in some tension with the moral point of view, even with considerably less stringent forms of it than the utilitarians' impartial benevolence. I doubt that we shall ever find a way to dispel totally the tension between prudence and morality, even if what I said in the last chapter about their penetrating one another is true.

One might hope that the tension could be reduced if we would, as some utilitarians might say we should, make impartial benevolence our central project; then one could accomplish something with one's life (a prudential value) by behaving impartially (a moral ideal). But this would be merely to realize one prudential value at the expense of many others—at the expense, say, of deep personal relations, of many forms of enjoyment, and, if this project takes much of one's time, of a lot of understanding. The tension arises even within the aim of impartially maximizing the good. A world in which everyone's life was as good as possible would be a world in which people were full of commitments. The impartial ideal, then, would be a world populated by agents incapable of promoting the impartial ideal. And what one comes to see as one's own individual form of flourishing becomes a large part of what one is; it combines many of the strands of one's personal identity. One's concern for one's own flourishing is not separate from one's concern for the survival of one's individual self. That is why Bernard Williams sees in the demands of impartial maximization of good a threat to a person's 'integrity', which, if the person lets it go far, becomes tantamount to 'suicide'. It is also why, in his autobiography, John Updike says: 'We are social creatures but, unlike ants and bees, not just that; there is something intrinsically and individually vital which must be defended against the claims even of virtue.'[1] Somehow, these two parts of ethics, the demands of others and the goal of individual flourishing, must be rendered, if not entirely harmonious, at least combinable in one normative point of view, and in one personality.

2. *The limits of the will*

Moral rules must mesh with human motivation. One cannot ask for what the human frame cannot deliver. I may certainly ask you to toss a lifebelt in order to save a stranger who has fallen into the sea, but not to sacrifice your life to do it. This brings us up against an empirical question on which most of our ethical beliefs rest, but which we largely ignore: What are the limits of human motivation?

Evolution has planted in us both crude self-interest and limited altruism.[2] We, like other animal species, defend ourselves with a tenacity that we do not display over many others. Our form of consciousness itself reflects the primacy of self-interest: our perceptions of our own pleasure and pain have a unique vividness to our minds and privileged link to our motivation;[3] our own everyday concerns fill our field of attention, the concerns of others appearing faintly at the periphery. It is true that there is genetic bonding to a few others. Many species, humans among them, are capable of great self-sacrifice, especially to protect offspring. But how can we expect beings like that, profoundly self-interested and of very limited altruism, to be capable of complete impartiality, counting everybody for one and nobody for more than one?

One obvious answer is that we can increase people's knowledge; we can make them appreciate far more fully and vividly the plight of others.[4] It is the approach of charities. We know how one photograph of a starving child can make tens of thousands reach for their cheque-books. Still, I doubt that the problem could be just a deficit in knowledge. Well-intentioned famine-relief workers, whose field of vision is filled with starving victims, no doubt make great sacrifices to help them, but do not generally sacrifice themselves to the point where their marginal loss equals the others' marginal gain. And the explanation cannot just be that anyone who helps others must keep healthy or wealthy enough to go on helping. It is true that there are often good impartial-maximizing reasons for those aiding to have more than those aided, but relief workers generally do not sacrifice themselves to that point either. And I find it hard to think that it is because their knowledge is still somehow incomplete or faint. To see the problem as simply one of knowledge does not take the full measure of its difficulty.

A more hard-headed answer is to impose some stiff behaviour modification. We should not mistake limitations that arise merely from social conditioning for genuine limitations in human nature. Anyway, human nature is not itself unmalleable. We are naturally partial; but so are we naturally aggressive and carnivorous, and no one suggests that those two features of human nature are not proper subjects for drastic moral demands. It is the approach of armies. In time of war, hundreds of thousands of perfectly ordinary people go off to defend their country at the risk of their lives. If military training can motivate them to go into battle, could not a well-conducted moral training do something comparable for us? In most cases, though, soldiers can be brought to accept great potential danger, I suspect, out of fear of the sergeant-major or a court martial or of being shamed in front of their mates. This suggests that we could, similarly, institute a kind of neighbourhood Red Guard to train us as children and to keep us up to moral scratch thereafter. It would be a terrible price to pay. We are willing to pay a comparable price in an emergency such as war, because of the exceptional importance of what is at stake. But perhaps we ought to think that what is at stake in morality is equally important.

But there are two different sorts of doubts about that whole Red Guard enterprise. First, to produce moral action by fear denies an agent autonomy, and loss of autonomy is the loss of an essential component of morality, at least as most of us now conceive of morality. Can we, in the name of morality, so substantially undermine morality? Anyway, second, the Red Guard approach would not work. Think what forces are gathered on the other side. Our propensity to form bonds of love and affection are vastly stronger than our propensity to eat meat. We think that our personal relations and our commitments to certain causes are central to a good life. These beliefs are not only common, but also, I should say, sound. And some sound ethical beliefs are, simply because they are sound, very likely to be persistent and recurrent, especially now that societies are much harder to isolate from one another. And these are attachments that cannot be entered into and exited from at will. We could, of course, try to suppress these commitments or alter these beliefs about the good life, but we are unlikely to succeed for long. The Red Guard enterprise aims at an unsustainable state. Many Chinese children who were model products of the Cultural Revolution turned up in the tents in Tiananmen Square.

Yet another answer is that, besides increasing knowledge and remoulding agents, we should give them a more inspiring goal. This is religion's answer. It is also, I take it, Iris Murdoch's answer.[5] Modern moral philosophy, she thinks, is unambitious. It sets modest goals; it assumes that our psychological capacities are puny. But goals and capacities are causally connected. Noble aims can turn egoism into something approaching altruism. The good, she says, is 'what makes a man act unselfishly in a concentration camp'.[6] And Jesus set the unmodest goal, 'Be ye therefore perfect'.

Are there any such transforming goals? If I thought that I was created by God, that my bodily life was an illusory passage to eternal bliss, that my flourishing consisted in the extinction of my own ego, and if I had the psychological support of a community of believers living the same sort of life, then I could probably make sacrifices that I cannot now make. I might also hope for some transformation of my will through divine grace. But I do not, nor do many religious believers, think that. My, and their, conception of human flourishing is nothing like that. Murdoch's own view of the goal of moral life is something like Plato's Form of the Good, and she sees it as having a magnetic power akin to many religious conceptions.[7] Perhaps it is best to see what she calls the 'sovereignty' of good as something not unlike selflessness or impartiality. But that goal, though inspiring, is not inspiring enough to transform motivation in the necessary way (at least, that is what I concluded a moment ago). The goals that might transform it I see no reason to adopt; and the goals that I see reason to adopt do not transform it.

Most of us agree that 'ought' implies 'can'. What we disagree about is exactly what sort of 'can't' it must be to defeat 'ought'. How unconditional does the 'can't' have to be? It is undeniable that some rare human beings sacrifice themselves for others. So they can. So humans can. So *we* can. And so the question, Ought we?, comes back to challenge us. At Auschwitz Father Maximilian Kolbe volunteered to take the place of another prisoner in a punishment detail, and went to his death. But that Father Kolbe, with his religious beliefs, could sacrifice himself does not show that we, with very different metaphysical beliefs, can too. In any case, we do not need to look to religious believers for cases of

self-sacrifice.[8] Hundreds of students in Tiananmen Square autonomously went on hunger-strike, and were prepared to die 'to fight
for the life that's worth living'.[9] But they were in special circumstances. They saw their lives as blighted, as not worth living.[10]
They saw an opportunity to change things, even if at a great cost
to themselves, and when they gave up hope of change, they gave
up the hunger-strike too. Certainly people in exceptional circumstances can do exceptional things. Some mothers, when their
children are threatened, can raise themselves to such emotional
intensity that they acquire powers that they do not normally have.
The hunger-strikers had despair over their lives, hope that they
could make a breakthrough, and the electric atmosphere of Tiananmen Square. But I doubt that we can use what people are capable
of at the pitch of excitement as evidence of what they are capable
of day in, day out, which is what a moral life needs. One special
circumstance would be impending disaster. We expect great sacrifices if the alternative is dire enough: I ought, I think, to accept
my own death to stop a lunatic getting to the nuclear button. That
the threat is so appalling should make motivation follow more
naturally.

What kind of 'can't', then, defeats 'ought'? There is 'can't absolutely': the human frame cannot deliver such-and-such. But
one certainly cannot maintain that complete impartiality is impossible in this absolute sense: history provides too many counter-
examples. Then there is 'can't if one is living a prudentially good
life in a non-oppressive society'. But this would be a claim about
the limits of the human will given some fairly hefty ethical restrictions. Still, there is a lot of ground between these two senses of
'can't', and the relevant sense, it seems to me, lies somewhere
there. Ethics must call on fairly settled dispositions. The dispositions must suit one for the variety of demands that life—in the
particular society that one is in and in the most important roles
that one is likely to play there—will make on one. Ethics must
presuppose a sustainable social order—sustainable given the material circumstances of our life and, especially, given what is most
enduring in human nature. The most relevant sense of 'can't',
therefore, seems to me to be this: can't by someone in ordinary
circumstances with suitable, settled dispositions in a sustainable
social order.[11] And the conditions attaching to this sense of 'can't'
do not set up great demands on understanding. Most of us have

to be prepared to raise children, or at least to have successful relations with other people, and more generally to be loyal and co-operative members of a community, and to care enough about our work to be productive. In short, we must live ordinary human lives; we must largely live as, anyway, we were going to live. A few people may turn out quite different from this; a very few of them, the ones who salvage some sort of sanity, might even be capable of effective impartial concern for all. But what is in the accessible psychological repertoire of the minute exception may well not be in the repertoire of the vast majority of human beings. In any case, none of us would be willing to raise our children to be utterly impartial; we should want to raise them to be capable of love and affection for those around them—that is hard enough. We should not know how to produce someone emotionally detached to that extreme degree, yet sane. We are incapable of such fine-tuning. We should be too likely simply to produce an emotional wreck.[12]

Many will think that I am overstating my case. For instance—and this is a common view—one could see impartiality as an admittedly unattainable, yet not pointless, ideal, an ideal that would have the good effect of making us stretch further than we otherwise would. When Jesus said, 'Be ye therefore perfect', he must have known that we should always remain largely imperfect, but that we might still find some point in trying for perfection. But 'try' implies 'think that one has a chance of doing'. The trouble is that we have no reason to think that we can, in the relevant sense, be perfect.

One might instead concede that we cannot act impartially at certain times of life—say, in the midst of child-rearing—but hold out for there being other times—say, in youth and old age, without entanglements—when we can. But that seems to assume a degree of plasticity in human nature that is not there. The dispositions that best suit an adult for the variety of demands life is likely to make cannot be radically different from the dispositions of a teenager. Deep attachments to people, commitment to work, ambition, and loyalty cannot just appear when one is 20 or 25. If they are not already securely established well before then, they will never appear. Nor can one expect morally serious persons to become impartial in old age, when their entanglements have loosened. Many people find themselves moving in that direction quite naturally, but entanglements usually only loosen; they do not fall away entirely. And the psychological material is likely to be too firmly set by then. To make someone capable of total impartiality requires taking drastic measures early.

Then, certain philosophers will reject my reading, or perhaps any reading, of ' "ought" implies "can" '. The source of moral norms, they will say, is capacity-blind, but no less authoritative for that. Had we been in the crowd waiting for Moses to descend with the tablets, we could have *hoped* that God's commandments would not exceed our capacities, but it could only be a hope. What God commands we ought to do, whether or not we can. 'Can', therefore, cannot be a necessary condition for 'ought'. But the conclusion we should draw from this example is much less clear-cut than that. If what God commands and we are able to do are too far apart, then we face a radical problem: how are we to form any conception of how actually to live? God may not lose authority by asking for so much, but we lose any articulation of a practicable policy for action. One cannot, for the reason already mentioned, fall back on saying that we are simply to *try* our best, because what we know we cannot do, we cannot try to do either. Nor can we aim simply at coming as close as possible to the commands, because that leaves entirely unarticulated what such a life would look like and what sorts of policies and personalities would be most likely to realize it; the job of describing decent *human* behaviour would remain. Fortunately for the Jews, the Ten Commandments did not demand what humans could not supply; unfortunately for Christians, some remarks of Jesus seem to do that (and so set up the need to describe a decent human life, which the Christian tradition has spent much time attending to). It is not just religious ethics that may create this problem; any capacity-blind form of objective ethics—for example, some (but not all) forms of ethical realism—has the potential for doing it. I am now concerned with secular ethics, and I know of no persuasive form of capacity-blind objectivity. But I shall come back to this matter in the next chapter.

I shall break off the discussion here; this is an enormously complex empirical issue, and there is much more to say about it.[13] My own conclusion is that, even allowing for all the ways in which the will can be stretched, there are major limits to it: complete impartiality is beyond normal human capacity.

3. *The demands of social life*

I suggested earlier that the nature of prudential values leads us away from looking at consequences act by act. It is better known that the facts of social life do too.

As a group, we have to solve *co-ordination* problems. Often all of us in a group want the same thing, but we will not get it unless we harmonize our actions. For instance, we cannot repel the attack if we all rush to man the same post. We also have to solve the more taxing *co-operation* problems. Each of us may have an aim that we can bring off individually, but may end up realizing it more fully by collaborating with others. For instance, each of us wants to prosper, but would prosper more by co-operating with the rest. But in such cases what each of us puts in and takes out can vary a lot from person to person, so solutions are typically not as easy as with co-ordination problems. A famous example of a co-operation problem is the Prisoner's Dilemma.[14] When two persons find themselves in a situation that has the form of a Prisoner's Dilemma, or something close to it, they have to avoid landing up with the third-best outcome for each. The most to be hoped for from any device that both parties would accept willingly is that it would lead to the better of the symmetrical results, so we need something to ensure the second-best outcome for each. Even if one of the parties to the dilemma is impartially benevolent, and so ready for self-sacrifice, what that person would most want would still be the second-best outcome for each, because that is best overall. So, given human nature, individuals need help to bring about this result.

Hence ethics must take account of group actions. Part of the solution to Prisoner's Dilemmas is to look not at one's own acts occasion by occasion, but at what groups do—to think strategically, not tactically. The strategic outlook would tell us to do what is necessary—by means of agreements, conventions, institutions, education, persuasion, penalties—to hit on and sustain co-operation that is beneficial.[15] Merely by shifting to a strategic outlook, a consequentialist might sometimes agree to what is called a political solution to a Prisoner's Dilemma. We might all, for instance, agree on an inescapable system of taxation, or one with drastic penalties for cheaters. Still, it is well known that detection of cheaters often cannot be assured, or sanctions be made fully

effective, so political solutions are not always enough. Then we
need to supplement them with what is called a psychological solution. We might raise children to have strong moral inhibitions.
But this, too, is not always enough. Sometimes education is unsuc-
cessful. Anyway, even if everyone were impartially benevolent and
thinking strategically, we should often need to co-ordinate action
and to obtain reassurance that enough others are going to co-
operate in some way for co-operation actually to have the best
results, and also that not so many will co-operate that it would be
better if some of us struck out on independent beneficial paths of
our own. There is more to human nature than strategic moral
outlooks, and much of it comes to our aid in making co-operation
likely, and so rational. Many institutions and attitudes existed well
before humans rose to the level of self-consciousness that allows
moral reflection. The origins of the institution of property may
go as deep as a genetically based human correlate of animal ter-
ritoriality. They certainly include the natural tendency to see
ourselves in what we labour over, in the hardly fully conscious
movement of thought: 'It's my doing; I am now in it; it's mine.'
Facts about the limits of human motivation also shape the institution. We are people of limited altruism; we will work to benefit
ourselves and those close to us, but not to benefit just anybody.
And we find ourselves in certain social and economic relations.
We are not a small tribe; we are not linked hierarchically by personal ties. We are in a huge industrial society of strangers, and
that makes some distributive rules relevant and others irrelevant.
As a result, many of our social institutions are already in place;
moral philosophers do not, out of their own materials, have to
provide all the reasons and motives that go into constructing them.
They have, rather, to provide answers to such questions as, Should
we work for new forms of co-operation? and What in our institutions needs changing?

Many social institutions are obligation-generating. You prom-
ised, so you should do it. Since you are the parent, you ought to
look after the child. It is her property, so hands off. We live our
lives within a setting of morally essential social institutions, conventions, and practices, on the one hand, and of prudentially
essential personal commitments and involvements, on the other.
Together they constitute a complex structure of obligations and
rights. These social institutions (and personal commitments too)

are obligation-generating and rights-bestowing. These obligations and rights give each of us reasons to do things for specific groups: for members of our society but not for inhabitants of the world at large, for those inside our particular co-operative enterprises but not those outside them, and for our own families but not members of society at large. As a result, there will be many obligations to those who are close that do not exist to those who are distant. And they will be obligations of great weight, because the institutions generating them are responsible for most of the major goods of our lives. Unless we have reason to think that these social institutions are seriously defective, we have good reason to accept these obligations.

4. *The limits of knowledge*

The last force shaping norms that I shall mention (there are, of course, many more) is the limits of human knowledge. Some information is not just typically, but permanently, beyond our reach, and much of it lies at the heart of morality. For instance, it would be helpful if we could tell how beneficial alternative forms of important social institutions, such as property, are, but their enormous complexity will often defeat us in the end. It is not that we can never manage such calculations. We can certainly manage to assess the costs and benefits of smallish parts of large social institutions. And we can tolerably reliably, if not very precisely, assess the costs and benefits of a whole complex social institution if its successes and failures are fairly plain. We can also advance our knowledge by trial and error. We can try, say, a centrally planned economy, and we may in time discover that it is inferior to a market economy in the efficient transmission of information. But that would leave us with very different forms of market economy, still to be ranked and differing in their effects on the quality of life. The effects of an economic structure are pervasive and subtle; they shape, in ways that are often beyond our grasp, not only economic performance, but also political structures and personal relations—for instance, our sense of community, the extent of our altruism, and the forms of our competition. Many of the kinds of market economy will fall in a band in which, though they differ in their costs and benefits, we shall not be able to rank them. We shall be unable to rank them not just for the present, but probably in the future too; we should need advances not just in economics, which may be forthcoming, but also in our understanding of how whole societies work, how individual psyches work, and how the one affects the other. There are, it is true, degrees of ignorance. We do not need certainty in order to act; a reliable degree of probability is enough. But at times we shall not have even that. There will still be a wide band in which our ignorance defeats even such judgements of probability. If we are wise, we shall then recognize our limits and settle for living within, while also reforming, the society that seems generally satisfactory that we have inherited.[16] What will then lie behind the claim that we ought to do this or that will not (that is, not entirely) be the general good, but that this is the way our society happens to work. Some moral norms are shaped by our own social tradition; we certainly do not create all our norms from scratch, but nor can we pass them all in review to sanction them as 'probable bests'. We work with the moral materials we have got, changing what we can see needs changing.

Let me give one more example. The limits of 'ought' are fixed by, among other things, the limits of 'can'. But where are they? We do not now know where the limits of 'can' are, and I doubt that we ever shall, except in terms that will leave them still largely indeterminate. Despite our ignorance, we go on to form a picture of what a normal human agent can manage, which in turn determines our conception of what a moral agent must do. The picture is to some degree arbitrary, and so too are the corresponding 'oughts'. We should like to think that moral obligations are not arbitrary, but since the limits of knowledge are inescapable, so too is the arbitrariness. To what extent can I deny myself and my family in order to help the world's starving? Our large measure of ignorance about that, along with our ignorance about the value of various institutions and practices, means that we simply have to choose a policy for ourselves (say, to contribute a certain per cent of our gross income to famine relief) and then stick to it. The limits of knowledge leave arbitrariness and contingency a large role in determining what, morally, we should do: for instance, the arbitrariness of our policy on charity and the forces that happen to have shaped our particular institution of property.

5. *Beyond common sense: philosophy and the search for system*

These four forces shaping our norms explain a lot about common-sense morality. Common-sense morality permits partiality to particular persons, groups, and causes; it incorporates the rights and obligations that arise from many of our social roles; it tailors moral demands to our capacities. And, importantly, it provides no all-embracing system for our various, apparently independent standards: they seem to emerge here and there from quite separate considerations—from our institution of property, from the relation of parent and child, from the role of a citizen—without any obvious single background consideration unifying them all.

System, however, is just what philosophy, it might be hoped, will introduce. It is one of philosophy's jobs to take us beyond common sense. But, as I shall come to shortly, the same facts about agents undermine many important ethical systems.

SOME COMPLEX MORAL IDEAS

1. *Where do moral norms come from?*

One source of moral norms is individual goods. We have the moral norm, Don't deliberately kill the innocent, because we value life.

But appeal to the value of life explains only so much. It would give us the simpler norm, Don't kill, which is too broad and too indiscriminate. Even the norm, Don't deliberately kill the innocent, is too indeterminate. It should not be interpreted as applying to a case of the following sort. (I am now going to consider several well-worn examples;[1] though they are old, I want in the end to say something new about them.) A runaway trolley rolls down a hill heading for a party of five standing on the track, unless you throw the switch next to you, thereby diverting it down another track on which only one person is standing. Of course, you must throw the switch, and the reason is: one dead, five saved. The value of life gives us a quite different norm for this case: Limit the damage.

But then should surgeons limit the damage by killing one person on the sly—a recluse, say, who would not be missed—to use the organs to save the lives of five desperately ill patients?[2] The numbers are the same: one dies, five live. Overall value has been promoted. Still, most of us hold that our duty to respect the life of the recluse is stronger than reference simply to the number of lives at stake will explain. The prohibition against killing, we think, applies here, though not in the trolley case. But why?

2. *Human limitations and the problem of scope*

Part of the answer, I think, is this. If you are standing by the switch as the trolley roars down the slope, your moral situation is very simple: is the damage to be small (one dead) or large (five dead)? The salient policy in the situation, the only rational policy, is, Limit the damage. The same is true, for instance, if my plane is going to crash, and all I can do is either let it carry on toward a town or steer it into the countryside; moral life is, at that point, exceedingly simple: better fewer dead. And the policy, Limit the damage, is modest in two ways. It makes no great demands on knowledge: the policy is obvious. And it involves no ambitious programme of action: we respond whenever, in exceptional circumstances, our hand is forced.

There is nothing like that modesty in the transplant case. Instead of reacting, when forced, the surgeons' policy is to go out into the world to find opportunities to limit the damage—that is, to promote preservation of life generally. And a policy like that makes enormous demands on knowledge. It also spreads naturally through life. If the surgeons do it today, why not tomorrow? If this group of surgeons does it, why not others? If surgeons do it, why not, say, politicians when their moral sums come out the same? And, typically, we cannot know in the transplant case, even to a reliable degree of probability, what will most promote values. The case is far from simple. The surgeons cannot know the consequences of killing the recluse. They cannot know whether, or how widely, people will learn what they have done. They cannot know how much fear and mistrust that knowledge will produce. They cannot do the calculation of total benefits against total costs. In any case, we are concerned now not with a particular case but with a policy. To do the calculations of costs and benefits if everyone—other groups of surgeons, politicians, and the rest of us—became entrepreneurs in life promotion is far beyond us. Anyone who aspires to a moral life based on such calculations aspires to God-like knowledge. 'Ought' implies 'can'. Morality is confined to the sphere of human capability. We are used to the fact that our physical and psychological capacities are limited, but so is our understanding. Moral norms are shaped for agents with all those limitations. So it is not surprising that we should use the norm, Limit the damage, in the trolley case and the norm, Don't deliberately kill the innocent, in the transplant case. Those are the appropriate norms for the likes of us.

One thing that alarms us about the transplant case, I say, is that the surgeons would be 'playing God'. Why would you not also be 'playing God' if you threw the switch for the trolley? Your role in the trolley case would be, I say, a relatively modest, un-God-like one. You are choosing, it is true, who will die, which seems a pretty God-like thing to do, but you are not arrogating to yourself anything approaching omniscience. The principle, Limit the damage, is modest just because of its salience, its obvious reasonableness, in those cases. The transplant case is different, I think, not just because the surgeons are deciding who is to die (that happens in the trolley case too), but because, in so doing, they are pretending to know that this is the best policy. They are setting themselves up as omniscient dispensers of justice in a situation in which there is no salient, obviously reasonable policy. No one, short of God, could see the best policy—even if the best came down simply to what produced most good for society at large and in the long run. So my suggestion is this. One thing that is objectionable about the surgeons' behaviour is not their intervention in the naturally unfolding course of events, but their pretension to be dispensing justice in doing so. Moral norms are shaped for us, with all our limitations. There are no moral norms outside the boundary set by our capacities. Ethics, particularly the ethics studied in modern universities, strikes me as often too ambitious. It usually fails to operate with a realistic conception of human agency. Ethics cannot do better for us in the transplant case than come up with norms for agents like us in the world so far as we are able to know it. One such norm is, Don't deliberately kill the innocent. And it takes an extreme case—some case, for instance, that is simple enough for another moral policy to be salient (though not error-proof)—for us to be justified in setting that norm aside. It would take a runaway trolley, or a plane headed for a crash.

3. *An objection*

There is an obvious objection to what I have just suggested. Granted that we need to conduct our moral life largely by appeal to norms (the objection goes), and that they must command a psychologically deep respect, and that the norm, Don't deliberately kill the innocent, is one of them. Nearly everyone accepts that. What is contentious, though, is how exceptions to the norm arise. It is not impossible that, by some fluke, the surgeons did know that no one would ever discover that they had killed the recluse. The recluse, let us say, is ill already, is on the surgeons' operating table for a high-risk operation, and can be finished off without arousing the least suspicion. True, their justification for killing the recluse could not stop there. Their justification is the promotion of most value, so the surgeons would need to know the values in prospect well into the possible futures of each of the six persons involved. But that, though increasing the fluke, is not quite impossible either; the surgeons might know something about the quality of life of the six—they are, after all, their patients. And anyway, our knowledge in the trolley case is far from complete. The five standing on the one track might be notorious Mafia hit men, and the one on the other track might be Mother Teresa. It is, none the less, right for you to throw the switch, because the probabilities of your successfully limiting the damage are so high. But by fluke the surgeons' knowledge could be even more reliable. So, it cannot be limitations on knowledge that make the difference between the two cases.

Now this objection directs our attention to a fluke—the surgeons' happening to know the costs and benefits. But the nature of our moral life is not determined by flukes. Hard cases make bad law; they also make bad moral norms. The norm, Don't deliberately kill the innocent, arises initially from the great value that we attach to life. But there is the further question as to how values such as life can enter human thought and action. Given the nature of agents, the role for these values in our lives is for us generally to respect them, not promote them. By 'respecting' life I mean primarily, but not solely, not oneself taking innocent life; by 'promoting' life I mean bringing about its preservation by any means open to one.[3] We typically cannot know, even to a reliable degree of probability, what will most promote life. Such God-like disposal of the affairs of the world is not our role. Ours is the more modest one of respecting life. That must be our general approach, and once we make it that, we cannot enter into and exit from such respect at will. Moral life, in certain ways, is bound to be deeply conservative. It will be conservative because of the centrality of deep feelings and attitudes. And it will be conservative because of the limitations of knowledge. In fluke circumstances in which we think we can determine the costs and benefits, we still only *think* that we know them. We are held back by both deep feelings and deep scepticism. We therefore demand that any exceptions to an important norm have an especially clear justification. We do not have to pitch the standards of justification so high that only something as thoroughly obvious as the trolley case or the plane case will do. We might be prepared to accept euthanasia in certain circumstances or obstetricians' sometimes killing the baby to save the mother. But these cases are still a long way from justifying the surgeons' killing the recluse in the transplant case.

4. *Other cases*

There will, of course, be cases less obvious than the trolley and plane cases. But the cases in which we can decide that it would be all right to set aside the norm, Don't deliberately kill the innocent, would be close to the trolley and plane cases in their relative simplicity. Think of the few situations in which a good person might deliberately take an innocent life:[4] for instance, smothering a baby whose cries would give away our hiding-place to the Gestapo, or eating the cabin-boy to keep at least some of the survivors of the shipwreck alive (in one version because the cabin-boy happens to have the worst chance of survival, in another because he happens to draw the short straw in a lottery to which they all agree). These cases are not as simple as the trolley or plane cases. The cabin-boy case is quite a bit more complex: if the Gestapo find the hiding-place, everyone, the baby included, will die, whereas the survivors of the shipwreck are not certain to die (they might be spotted in time by a passing ship). But the situations may be simple enough, and the probabilities extreme enough even in the cabin-boy case, for the policy of limiting the damage to apply.

There are more difficult cases. In both the smothered baby case and the cabin-boy case, all the persons involved are, if not certain to die, at least seriously threatened. But imagine a situation closer to the transplant case. (It is a variation on another scenario of recent moral casuistry.) A rock fall blocks the exit to a grotto, trapping six tourists inside, and the rising tide threatens to drown them. They find a small hole in the roof, but the first of their party to reach it is the fattest, who gets stuck and cannot move backward or forward. Workers outside have no equipment to save them apart from a small stick of dynamite, not enough to blast a new hole, but enough to blast the fat tourist out of the old hole. (On one variation of the example, there are no workers there, but one of the trapped tourists has the dynamite.) The fat tourist would not otherwise die; with enough time the workers could fetch drills to enlarge the hole, but the water is rising too fast for that to help the others. The fat tourist pleads not to be blown up; the other five plead to be saved as the rising waters reach their necks. Should the workers kill one to save five? They would probably be paralyzed by the very thought of blowing up the fat tourist. It would be excusable, in ways even admirable, if they could not bring themselves to do it. But would it be morally wrong if they did it? Unlike the transplant case, there is no policy at stake here. The workers' dilemma is unique in their lives, and is most unlikely ever to occur in ours, whereas the surgeons' opportunity is all too repeatable. It is probably because the grotto case presents none of those worries that we are more inclined to think that it would not be morally wrong, even if appalling, to blow up the fat tourist.

5. The possibility of system: (a) utilitarianism

I have been speaking of two moral norms, one a prohibition, Don't deliberately kill the innocent, and the other a positive instruction, Limit the damage. Each is understood in a way that keeps it from trespassing on the territory of the other. The story of these norms that I have told so far has drawn only on an account of well-being and a conception of agents and their social setting. It is hard to detect in the story so far any single, ultimate principle underlying all moral norms, as utilitarians find, or any one consideration, such as the sort of rational requirement that Kantians find, that might bring system to ethics.

But that is counting without philosophy. Does *it* not introduce system? The same facts about agents, I think, undermine certain important ethical systems. I want to take a quick look now at three major traditions in moral philosophy: utilitarianism, deontology, and virtue ethics. But before I do, I want to make clear the spirit in which I shall do it. One cannot say anything definitive about a rich philosophical tradition in a few pages—or in a book, for that matter. Rich traditions, by definition, have too many resources for that. The philosopher's self-indulgence is over-generalization; we get a bright critical idea about one or two forms of some view, and elevate it into a knock-down argument against all forms. Rational criticism is certainly possible in ethics; it is just not easy to be conclusive with traditions that are both so deep and so incompletely formulated. I am tempted to say that, for secular ethics, it is early days, except for my inability to see how later days will be so different. Where will the revolution in our position come from? Still, it is true that we lack satisfactory statements of our options in ethics. So far as utilitarianism goes, we are only now again questioning what an adequate account of human well-being might be, and the distinction between direct and indirect utilitarianism was drawn in any explicit way only recently, and remains insufficiently explored. As for deontology and virtue ethics, they are in a worse state; they have been formulated in only the scrappiest way. We find it hard to know what we are meant to choose among. At this stage, we can hope only that criticism might give us a better, rather than a worse, hunch about where it is most promising to look. I want merely to explain the source of my own doubts about these three traditions and why, on balance, I prefer to look elsewhere.

First, then, utilitarianism. An obvious doubt about a direct form of utilitarianism is whether persons can have the commitment to their family, their pursuits, and their community that they must have for private and public life to go well, yet be able to drop these commitments whenever utility calculation beckons. We stand loose enough from some undertakings to retain that degree of freedom, but not from the central commitments of our private and public lives. Some commitments do not leave us able, occasion by occasion, having reviewed all actions that are in some sense within human capacity before dispositions have been formed, to choose the best; some will not leave us with time to notice chances for doing more good; others, especially to other persons, will not leave us able to take such chances even if we see them. Direct utilitarians can respond to these facts of life by including among their options becoming deeply committed. But to opt that way would be, for them, subversive; it would undercut, over a large swathe of the moral domain, their distinctive form of deliberation.

By contrast, an indirect form of utilitarianism can concede that the moral norms and relations that for the most part govern our lives are much like the ones that we find in common-sense morality; all that it must insist on is that they be sanctioned by the highest-level moral consideration, the impartial promotion of interests. It proposes that we should act in accord with the norms, or from the feelings, that would promote interests in the whole society in the long run. But my doubt about indirect utilitarianism is whether we could often perform the tremendously large-scale cost–benefit calculations that it requires, or even often arrive at probabilities reliable enough for action. We can do these calculations in fairly extreme or fairly small-scale cases, but usually not otherwise.[5] Something else will then have to be at work producing determinate moral norms and relations. Such norms and relations must be tailored to fit the human moral torso. They are nothing but what such tailoring produces. There are no moral norms outside the boundary set by our capacities. There are not some second-best standards, standards made for everyday use by agents limited in knowledge and will, and then, underlying them and sanctioning them, true standards, standards that make no compromise with human frailty. A moral standard that ignores human capacities is not an 'ideal' standard, but no standard at all.

Utilitarians might, at this point, object that impartially promoting interests is not, in any case, meant as an action-guiding principle. There is an important distinction between a decision procedure (how we should go about deciding how to act) and a criterion (what in the end makes an act right or wrong). Perhaps a doctor is best advised to follow certain procedures in diagnosing and treating patients—best advised because those procedures have best results overall, though not necessarily in each case. But the criterion for successful medical practice—health—is clear, and is independent of any sensible diagnostic procedures. Perhaps, similarly, the impartial promotion of the good is properly seen not as the consideration that we use to decide what to do, but as the criterion of our moral practice.

But I doubt that this reply helps utilitarianism. Although criterion and decision procedure can indeed diverge, they may not, I think, get far apart from one another. Our decision procedures will, of course, be restricted by our capacities, but any criterion for a human practice cannot become too remote from them without losing its standing as a criterion. Health can be a criterion for

medical practice, because doctors can usually both act to bring it
about, or come as close to it as present techniques allow, and in
time find out whether they have succeeded. In parts of moral life
we can also eventually find out the important consequences of
our acts, but in many other parts we never do. What most promotes interests is often permanently beyond our reach. Then a
would-be 'criterion' like that can play no role, not even that of a
criterion. Our moral life cannot start from such an all-sanctioning
background principle. We have to conduct it with what is within
our reach. One might—and the capacity-blind objectivists that I
spoke of in the last chapter do—flatly deny my claim that there
are knowledge constraints on a criterion. The criterion in morals,
they say, is independent of human capacities; it is the sort of thing
to be discovered by us; we may hope that it does not outstrip our
powers of knowledge, but that can only be a hope. But this form
of objectivism seems to me to lack support.[6] And if the criterion
were to outstrip our knowledge, then it could play no role in our
moral life; it would leave indirect utilitarianism in need of some
new, yet unknown, standard for sanctioning the rules of our decision procedure. This objectivist move is so drastic that it punches
a large hole in utilitarianism that the theory has no obvious resources to fill.

This is why the obvious utilitarian reply to my line of thought
is not, I think, strong enough. The reply goes like this. We utilitarians are perfectly able to accept any facts about human nature
or the workings of society, including (if they turn out to be true)
your claims. We can, for instance, accept that moral life has to be
conducted by appeal to fairly specific standards, in just the ways
you say and for just the reasons you give. We shall simply incorporate all this in the utilitarian calculation. Our question then becomes: What set of rules and dispositions will most promote
interests, given agents of such-and-such a nature and a society that
works thus-and-so? But this reply does not meet the strength of
the claim that I have made. My suspicion is that *this* calculation is
beyond us, and that our moral life cannot therefore rest on it.
Utilitarians cannot admit that our ignorance justifies the sort of
reliance upon tradition that I have defended. That concedes too
much; it concedes that even indirect utilitarian thought is out of
place in much of the centre of moral life. The crux is how often
utilitarian thought is squeezed out. A few times would not matter;

often would. If it is squeezed out of quite a large part of moral
life, if there prove to be many situations in which the calculation
of utilities cannot be done to a sufficient degree of reliability, then
does enough remain to be called 'utilitarianism'? That is not a
rhetorical question. It seems clear that *sometimes* utility calculation,
even to a reliable degree of probability, is beyond us. And in
moral life it may not be of much use that we can in future extend
our knowledge, say by trial and error. If it takes virtually one's
whole life to establish that one has tried the wrong policy, one
cannot live one's life again. And if one's error has hurt others,
they cannot live their lives again either. What we have to decide
is just how often tolerably reliable utility calculations are beyond
us, and how central those failures are in moral life. What one
finds will, to some extent, depend upon the kind of utilitarian
one is. If one thinks (as I do) that the most plausible form of
utilitarianism is a highly indirect one, then at the centre of one's
moral thought will be some such question as: What set of rules
and what set of dispositions would, if they were to prevail in one's
society, produce most utility over society at large and in the long
run? But that is just the sort of question likely to defeat answer.
We may know enough to identify fairly obviously inadequate rules
and dispositions, but there will be many left that we cannot rank.
And it is in the wide band that they would constitute that many
of the hard choices in morality—choices, say, about the particular
form that respect for life should take—would have to be made.
Utilitarianism seems to turn ethics into a project that fits badly the
agents who are meant to carry it out. The ambitions of utilitarian
rationality seem too great.[7]

6.(*b*) *Deontology*

It is better to accept that some moral norms and relations have an
authority of their own, independent of their promoting the good.
That is a point that deontologists—correctly, I think—insist on.
But they explain it by introducing a further *moral* standard: they
say that, in addition to promoting individual goods, and in addition to any overarching moral consideration such as giving each
person his due, there are underivative and fairly specific moral
permissions and prohibitions, or at least moral considerations pro

and con. And some deontologists add that we can often gauge the relative moral weight of these considerations, thus opening up prospects of system.

One worry about deontology, a worry that many deontologists share, is the number of places where its account turns mysterious. How do we identify these deontological standards? An old answer is: by intuition. But deontologists have to show that these identifications are different from arbitrary expressions of like and dislike. There is the same problem with the identification of prudential values, as I discussed earlier. We need standards of correctness, as well as an error theory, for identifying both prudential values and deontological standards. Though the project for prudential values is in a primitive stage, there is a reasonable hope that it can be carried out. It is much less clear that it can be in the deontological case. And nobody seems to know quite how to handle deontological constraints, how they work with other elements of moral thought. They threaten a breakdown in moral reasoning. To make these constraints absolute would be puzzling; we cannot see why these considerations should have supreme weight. But to make them less than absolute leaves us with the puzzle of the turning-point: if enough good justifies putting the constraint aside, how much is enough? Of course, mystery is not the prime defect of theory; better a mysterious adequate account than a non-mysterious inadequate one.

Still, one mystery that deontologists cannot allow to stand is how we are to identify the independent, fairly specific moral standards that they posit. Deontologists of all sorts posit such standards: absolutists, who identify exceptionless prohibitions; near absolutists, who identify prohibitions that only a catastrophe can set aside; pluralists, such as W. D. Ross, who identify several potentially conflicting prima-facie duties, one's duty overall being the most stringent one in the circumstances; and pluralists who identify not the sort of general principles that Ross had in mind (which, for Ross, always have weight), but moral features that arise from and must be balanced in a particular case.

Some deontologists, therefore, identify acts that are prohibited in virtue of their *kind*.[8] And they seek to dispel the mystery by bringing the kind under a description that will itself help make clear what is wrong. But in many cases it has proved extremely hard to find a satisfactory description. In the transplant kind of case the description usually offered is 'deliberately killing the innocent'. Yet the sailors deliberately kill the innocent cabin-boy, and the workers deliberately dynamite the innocent fat tourist. Perhaps the most common approach is to identify prohibited kinds and then offer a further account of exceptions—say, competing obligations that outweigh the prohibition. But we cannot respond that in the cabin-boy and grotto cases the wrongness of the act is outweighed by the amount of good at stake, because the amount of good, five lives saved, might be the same as in the transplant case. And it is hard to identify any other kind that does better. One could, for instance, use the terms 'murder'[9] or 'unjust killing'[10] for any case of deliberately killing the innocent that had the required moral status. But then the descriptions 'murder' and 'unjust killing' would not identify the ground of its having that status, but would presuppose a ground that was still unidentified.

Some deontologists take a different tack. Instead of identifying a kind of act, they identify a kind of intention. What are prohibited are acts that proceed from an evil intention, that violate, say, moral respect for persons.[11] That approach may be able to distinguish the transplant case from the trolley case: perhaps in diverting the trolley you can be said to foresee the death of the one person standing on the track but not to intend it, whereas the surgeons intend the recluse's death. Here the approach is to give a sensitive enough account of the prohibited kind that what on other accounts would be exceptions are not prohibited in the first place. Still, the sailors intend the cabin-boy's death, and the workers intend the fat tourist's death. Both the doctrine of double effect and the principle of respect for persons have been developed with an ingenuity that has extended their application to a wide range of cases. But my own belief is that there remain cases that they cannot explain adequately, and that, at some point in extending their application, it begins to look very much as if whether an act is justified is determining whether the required sort of intention or respect is present, and not, as deontology needs, the other way around.[12]

Some deontologists try yet another tack. What distinguishes the transplant case from the trolley case, they propose, is the violation of a right.[13] The surgeons infringe the recluse's right to life, whereas you do not infringe the right of the one person standing on the track by diverting the trolley. I suppose that there is such a thing as a right to life, but its content is notoriously unclear. Many would say that the right to life is infringed if the surgeons kill the recluse but not if, instead, they let their five patients die. But is the right infringed if I do not bother to toss a lifebelt to a drowning child? Perhaps the right is not infringed in the smothered-baby or cabin-boy cases, simply because the probability is so high of their all dying otherwise, baby and cabin-boy included, that these cases, like the trolley case, fit under the norm, Limit the damage. But the fat tourist would certainly survive; in that way the grotto case is like the transplant case. Many would also say that the fat tourist's right to life would be violated if the workers resorted to dynamite, but that the right would be overridden by the other five lives at stake. But if that is so—if that is where we should draw the line around the right to life—then it cannot be the right that explains the moral difference between the grotto case and the transplant case, because the same overriding condition is present in both. What we need is a substantive theory of rights that will come out with the result that the right to life is infringed in the transplant case but not in the cabin-boy or grotto cases. No one has yet developed such a substantive theory, and I myself cannot see how any development would ever end up there.[14]

But what exactly would be wrong if deontologists were to stick to their guns? What if they were perfectly prepared to live with the consequences of a prohibition on deliberately killing the innocent: one must not eat the cabin-boy, or smother the baby, or blow up the fat tourist?

What, to my mind, would be wrong is that we could not then supply the background that the prohibition needs in order to be intelligible. To be intelligible, it must have some links, even if tenuous and indirect, with interests.[15] We could not understand it as a prohibition apart from the great value that we attach to life. This is not at all a specifically utilitarian point; it is a general requirement. What commands protection must be able to strike us as worth protecting. What demands respect, we must be able to see as respectable. How could murder acquire moral status independently of the havoc it wreaks in human lives? It is the idea of deontological constraints floating entirely free of interests that is baffling, even incredible. Some writers have tried to anchor these constraints by appeal not to interests, but to the naturally repellent character of evil. If by murdering one person I could save two, and if I simply weighed up the interests at stake (one life against two), then I should, they think, be ignoring the intrinsically repellent character of evil; I should be swimming 'head on against the normative current'.[16] But talk of evil does not lessen the bafflement; evil cannot be free-floating either. It must connect with interests, if only to use them as one part of a many-sided account of why each separate person demands respect. And deontologists must also explain why prohibitions differ in strength—why, for instance, a ban on killing is more stringent than a ban on theft, the obvious explanation being that life is generally of greater value than property.

I think that most deontologists would be prepared to accept this loose sort of link between prohibitions and interests. What is characteristic of deontology is its denial that we are merely to *promote* the related values: one may not deliberately kill the innocent, even if more lives could be saved thereby. Values may have to enter the picture to make prohibitions intelligible, but some values are to be respected, not promoted.

But there is trouble here. Sometimes the value now acknowledged to be necessary for a prohibition's intelligibility disappears. For instance, in certain circumstances, nothing of what makes life valuable is to be found. A person near death may be suffering so intensely that everything else is blotted out—relations with other people, autonomy, reflection, dignity. Yet euthanasia comes under the ban; it is deliberately killing the innocent. It is not that one cannot make a ban on euthanasia intelligible in some other way— say, by appeal to God's will. But that way of making sense of it is not available to a secular ethics. For a secular ethics, the deontological account is left, at least for the present, with large holes. Merely shifting from absolute to non-absolute deontology does nothing at all to fill that theoretical gap; it just adds a further problem, the problem of the turning-point.

I have hardly exhausted the variety of forms of deontology, but let me stop here. Like utilitarianism, deontology seems to me to be over-ambitious. In both its systematic and its unsystematic forms, it assumes that a certain kind of rationality can be discovered in morality: that we can find features of the act or the agent to rationalize good conduct—that, for instance, we can find a formula, such as 'deliberately killing the innocent', to explain the difference between, on the one side, the transplant case and, on the other, the trolley and cabin-boy and grotto cases. And in its more systematic forms, it assumes that there are moral considerations to which we can attach weights that can be balanced against one another; indeed, in its most common variety, that there is a turning-point at which the good becomes large enough to outweigh the prohibition. In the end, the thing to say about this project is: it looks like too tall an order. It asks for more than we have now, and also for more than we have any reason to expect to acquire in future.

7.(c) Virtue ethics

Moral life must be a life that the likes of us can lead. The likes of us, I have said, must live by certain norms: prohibitions, instructions, permissions that are tailored to agents with our capacities. But, for the same reasons, as I touched on earlier, we must largely act from the informed feelings that make up so much of our moral life: sympathy, respect, loyalty, fidelity. These thoughts move us into the general neighborhood of virtue ethics.

Unless we find ourselves in extreme circumstances, we live within the network of moral relations that such informed feelings as loyalty and respect define. Such relations must also go some way toward explaining the force of the prohibition in the transplant case. The norm, Don't deliberately kill the innocent, rests on our respecting the great value of life. But what is at stake in the transplant case is not just respect for life, but respect for the recluse's standing as a centre of choice, as a determiner of what happens in the world, as an autonomous agent. In denying the recluse that, the surgeons would be denying him a value in the same league as life itself.

This case for the centrality of moral dispositions and relations does not make them second-best. It is not that we use consequentialist rationality whenever we can and fall back on dispositions and relations, for lack of anything better, when that rationality runs out. Respect for values—for life, for instance—is the only form that moral life can take over a fair amount of its domain; consequentialist rationality can enter only here and there. Moral dispositions and relations have standing not because they are sanctioned by an all-pervasive background consequentialist rationality;

to think so is greatly to exaggerate the powers of consequentialist rationality. In extreme circumstances it may be morally allowed to betray a trust or deliberately kill the innocent. It may be that, in those extreme circumstances, another moral standard becomes relevant, as I suspect it does, for instance, in the trolley and cabin-boy and grotto cases. But the fact that respect for agreements and respect for life do not get their importance solely from promoting interests explains a further belief of common-sense morality: namely, these forms of respect do not lose their importance when, for the sake of promoting interests, one is allowed to fail in respect. One who fails in respect, even when morality permits it, still partly fails morally and may rightly feel the need for regret, apology, or amends.

These thoughts move us, as I say, into the general neighbourhood of virtue ethics, though not yet, I think, all the way to it. Most moral views—indeed, all plausible ones—make the virtues important. So that is not enough to qualify those views as a form of what we nowadays call 'virtue ethics'. What is definitive of virtue ethics, I take it, is that it makes virtues not just important to, but also in some sense basic in, the moral structure: they are so deep in the structure that they can be said to generate or to animate the rest of it.[17] It need not make virtues fundamental in the whole structure of *values*—that position one might regard as reserved for the human good or flourishing, by reference to which the virtues are defined. But it places virtues deep in the *moral* structure, in the structure of our thought about what consideration we owe to others in particular circumstances: it makes the assessment of agents more basic than the assessment of actions. It explains what it is to act rightly in some situation in terms of doing what a virtuous person would do.[18]

The criterion for correct choice proposed by virtue ethics, therefore, is not a slate of general principles, but a person: our standard is a person with informed dispositions in wise balance. But this criterion cries out for clarification at two points. If virtues are dispositions of the *right* sort, how do we decide on the *right* sort? And how do we decide on the *right* balance between them?

Moral feelings, such as sympathy, compassion, and love, are well known to be able to lead us astray. Compassion can be just soft-heartedness; one can lend a hand when it would have been better to let the person cope alone. So the dispositions that are allied to virtues must, as virtue ethics itself says, go through much critical refinement. If compassion is a virtue, it must be different from soft-heartedness. But if we must find the *right* dispositions in the *right* balance with one another, then the criteria for *right* threaten to occupy the ground floor in the moral structure, kicking virtues upstairs.

Consider how the search for the right balance actually goes in a particular case. We have respect for life (that is what should make the surgeons stay their hand in the transplant case). We have concern for others (that is what should make you throw the switch in the trolley case). Respect for life, though, if it is to be of any use in ethics, must be made fairly determinate—vastly more determinate than the phrase 'respect for life' makes it. We must know more about when it imposes demands on us and the form they take. It is, for instance, potentially in competition with our concern for others, so we must get some fuller idea of the proper domain of each. We cannot hope to get a lot more help out of the background idea of what humans need, individually and socially, for the species to flourish. For it to flourish, we clearly need re-spect for one another's lives and benevolence. But the notion of human flourishing, having delivered itself of these two domains of excellence, does not seem able to take us much further toward fixing tolerably determinate boundaries for them. How would we get further? Well, what should we do if we have a dying patient in agony, for whom pain-killers have stopped working? We should have to balance the respect for life that generally stays our hand with the compassion for suffering that generally moves it. But the way we should go about striking the balance is by answering cer-tain questions. What is in the patient's interest? Did the patient leave any instructions? As this is not a one-off case, what changes in the doctor/patient relation would be likely to follow from a new policy? What limits should the new policy have? Can they ever be formulated in a way that the likes of us can satisfactorily follow? And so on—that is just the start of the list. Reliable answers to those questions might well refine further our sometimes conflict-ing dispositions of respect and compassion. But what would have done all the work are not our dispositions, but the answers to the questions. And they centre on many of the same considerations at work in exempting the cabin-boy and grotto cases from the ban on deliberately killing the innocent: namely, the promotion of human interests, the need to live largely, but not always, by norms, and the vital role of the limits of knowledge. It is hard to see, in what I have managed to single out so far about these cases, any reason for thinking that the virtues are fundamental in the whole moral structure.

What, in particular, is implausible is the form of virtue ethics that claims there to be an ideally virtuous person, whose dispositions are in perfect balance and who therefore is better able to perceive situations correctly, including features that general principles often fail to capture. This is another piece of over-ambition in ethical theory: the assumption that the likes of us could ever become sensitive enough to all the moral considerations at work in particular cases and to their proper weight for that sensitivity to be up to guiding our actions. This exaggerates both our sensitivities and the determinateness of the moral considerations available for us to be sensitive to. There is a limit to what we can hope for from a perception of particular moral features of cases: such determinate features can run out before we have a solution, and leave us clinging to a general norm. The best we can do in the transplant case is to stick to the policy of respecting life. The best we can do in the case of euthanasia is to find a formula that can be applied by the likes of us, allowing us thereby to shift certain cases from the ambit of the norm, Don't deliberately kill the innocent, to the norm, Limit the damage.

Let me stop here with virtue theory. This discussion, like the earlier ones, is much too quick to be conclusive. I make only a suggestion. I do not think that the prospects of carrying out the programmes of utilitarianism or deontology or virtue ethics are bright. I think that we are left with something much closer to common-sense ethics than they—at least in their more systematic or reductive versions—claim. I think that we are left with the sort of account of, say, the prohibition, 'Don't deliberately kill the innocent', that I gave earlier in this chapter.

But there is an obvious challenge to make to my own position. In raising doubts about other positions—utilitarianism, virtue ethics, and especially deontology—have I not resorted to piecemeal appeal to intuition? I began this book by saying that we should hope for a better method than that, and in the process of constructing what I see as a better method, I have depended, it seems, on the worse one. But I think that I have not, in any culpable way.

My point about piecemeal appeal to intuition, in any case, was not that it shows nothing, but that it is unclear how much it shows, and that we should not resign ourselves to it as our sole form of criticism unless we have to. Some of my doubts about deontology appeal to intuitions; others do not. I have at times appealed to core prudential values and to moral standards so close to them as to be, in effect, part of the core. But for the most part I have appealed to standards of knowledge and to the nature of agents. My main point about utilitarianism, deontology, and virtue ethics is not that they sometimes give bad advice (though that may also be true), but that they constitute programmes that cannot be carried out. They are, in one way or another, unrealistic. I cannot see how ethics can be all that they want it to be.

8. *My proposal*

My own view is that philosophers have not yet paid nearly enough attention to the nature of human agents. When we do, we find, I think, an explanation of the moral standards we have been talking about that gives them a standing that utilitarianism does not, but without resorting either to the further moral standards that deontology posits but has trouble finding or to the primacy of moral dispositions that virtue ethics claims but has trouble justifying.

I have said that the norm, Don't deliberately kill the innocent, holds sway in all but extreme cases, because it is the only norm suitable as a general policy for agents like us. My guess is that one obstacle to our accepting that conclusion is the myth of the morally right answer. We do not expect positive law always to have an answer: a situation may be so unusual that no law fits it, even that no legislator's intention fits it. We are prepared to accept the positive law as an inadequate, incomplete human creation, not always up to coping with the complexities of life. But underlying positive law, we think, there is an ideal form of law, moral law, endlessly refinable, universally applicable, and never at a loss for an answer (though we may be at a loss to make it out). But moral law is limited in much the same way, and for many of the same reasons, as positive law. The myth is that there is always the morally right answer. Sometimes moral norms conflict, and there is no background moral rationality to resolve the conflict. Sometimes we just have to stick to a moral norm, such as, Don't deliberately kill the innocent, despite all the nagging and, in a sense, rational worries weighing in on the other side—as in the transplant case— because that is the only kind of moral life open to us.

There is something else, I think, holding us back: the myth of the sufficiency of the moral. Purely moral considerations often leave us well short of determinate standards for action, and other considerations, for example, social agreement or convergence or tradition, have to be brought in to fill the gap. For instance, human rights have their moral grounding, I should say, in the great value that we attach to our status as persons, as agents. As persons, we deliberate about and choose our ends, and then act to realize them. Human rights are best seen, on this Enlightenment conception of them, as protections of the values associated with personhood: namely, our autonomously choosing a course through life, our having the basic wherewithal to achieve it, and others not blocking us. So one human right is a right to bodily integrity, because unless we have some security in our own bodies, we shall have no security of action. But where is the line defining that right to be drawn? Does that right bar the state from forcibly taking one of my kidneys for transplant? Does it also bar a particularly accommodating state from demanding a pint of my blood, which, it says, it will take in my own house while I sleep, leaving me to wake the next morning none the worse for it? What is clear is that, on its own, the relevant moral consideration—namely, the value of personhood—is not up to fixing a determinate line. The personhood consideration would not protect me against the accommodating state that was after my blood. It is not clear that it would protect me even against the state that was after my kidney; after all, what I should lose from a kidney extraction is only a few weeks for convalescence (if my remaining kidney packs in, there is a bank of them for me to have a transplant), and a few weeks convalescence will hardly destroy my personhood. But the trouble is that the personhood consideration, unsupplemented, draws nothing even approaching a determinate line. And if the line is very fuzzy, we may even be reluctant to say that a right yet exists. Its existence must, to some extent, depend upon its being a manageable, socially effective claim on others. So what sort of thing must we add to make it more determinate? A lot of practical considerations must go into fixing the line—such as how threateningly interventionist the political tradition of our particular society is, whether human nature is such that we should be well-advised to leave a large safety margin, how simple and obvious the line has to be, and so on.

So we should not think that there are always determinate moral norms underlying laws or other social standards, which provide us with the ideal to which laws or social standards must measure up. It is not that there will be no rational grounds for assessing laws and social standards, but that they will not be entirely moral in content. They might, instead, be in terms of social or psychological probabilities. I am inclined to say that it is often the other way around: that moral norms—that is, norms as far as purely moral considerations take them—are often highly indeterminate, and need some realistic picture of a satisfactory form of social agreement added to them to give them shape. Sometimes it is the law itself that will give them shape.[19] More often, though, it is some non-legal, moral consensus—or realistic prospect of consensus. In this further way, moral norms are like laws. It is often society, through its conventions and convergences and decisions, that defines them, and so brings them into existence.

We follow the norm, Don't deliberately kill the innocent, unless we find a tolerably clear area of exception—as there is with cases covered by the norm, Limit the damage. And there must be another area of exception, though its boundaries are hard to draw, for euthanasia. Legislators defining a policy on euthanasia have to face up to the fact that it will be applied by limited, temptable humans. Any legislation is bound to be a messy compromise with human nature and social needs. But it is not that behind a legislator's messy deliberation there is a moralist's purer thought. The two deliberations will be virtually the same: the same problems, the same compromises, the same vagueness and incompleteness.

I am saying that moral norms are like positive laws not in their content, but rather in the modes of thought used to arrive at them, and in the considerations central to that thought, especially the limitations of agents and the solutions to actual social problems. On the contrary, one would hope that the content of moral norms would often diverge from that of positive laws. One wants moral norms to provide grounds for criticizing laws; and so they can if those who think about ethics keep a step or two ahead of legislators. It is just that when those interested in ethics think about human rights or abortion or euthanasia, they shall have to think about the same messy variety of considerations that a legislator does. Our job in ethics is not to have thoughts radically different from theirs, but earlier on, or carried further, than theirs. For instance, there is nothing to stop us from reaching a feasible norm about euthanasia before legislators do (at least, legislators in the United Kingdom and the United States); and we can carry our deliberation to the highly specific or particular (say, in the cabin-boy case), whereas they, given the nature of the legislative exercise, cannot.

What I am suggesting is that there is no domain of the moral—that is, a kind of thinking that appeals to purely moral considerations and is capable on its own of producing a body of determinate conclusions that can guide life. A few determinate conclusions can be arrived at that way; the norm, Don't be cruel, is simple enough to be one. But many other moral norms, and important ones, will be too indeterminate to serve effectively as norms until we add various practicalities. Then there is only a wider domain—a kind of thinking in which the considerations are much more heterogeneous, more concerned with the possible, and more subject to compromise—the domain of the social.

9. *Ethical conservatism*

We have to make do without the extensive background rationality that most utilitarians and some deontologists think is available to us. They think that underlying our various moral standards there always is, in principle, a procedure for weighing the overall amount of good at stake or the relative stringency of the duties in play. But these sorts of all-pervasive background rationality, I think, prove impossible. At points we have to fall back on natural sentiment, on a variety of well-entrenched but unsystematic norms, and on tradition, which have to recommend them that they carry us from where an exclusively moral rationality drops us to where we must get.

The source of the moral prohibitions we have been considering is located, not exclusively but in no small measure, in the nature of agents. A consequence of this is that we are right to attach moral weight to certain common-sense distinctions—for instance, between *acting* and *omitting*, *doing* and *letting happen*, duties *not to harm* and duties *to aid*. We live by, and can only live by, the moral norms and relations that I have been speaking of, and they embody a form of these distinctions. But the source of the distinction lies, I suspect, in the nature of agents, not in the nature of two kinds of behaviour—acting and omitting, doing and letting happen, and so on.[20] And the same source yields the common-sense distinction between *duty* and *supererogation*. Any ethics works with an inevitably rough, arbitrary picture of the limits of the will. Often the best we can do is to adopt a correspondingly rough, arbitrary policy: say, pick some level of contribution to charity and abide by it, those doing markedly more thus going beyond the call of this ill-defined duty.

What I am saying, despite my invocation of tradition and common sense, is not especially conservative. It is certainly not anything like a wholesale defence of common-sense ethics, which has always had its inadequacies in the past, and must have them still. We have powerful forms of criticism available to us: appeals to utilities, to rights, to the nature of agents and of society. That there is no supreme background principle capable of bringing system to ethics does not mean that there are no less-than-supreme background principles capable of sustaining important criticism of our prevailing beliefs. To amplify this point, let me say something about the first of these critical resources, appeal to utilities.

Utilities are at the centre of the issue about euthanasia, and euthanasia is one place where common-sense ethics sorely needs change. Some cases of euthanasia are, I think, quite simple. When life has no value, when it is reduced to nothing but suffering, the prohibition on deliberately taking it loses its intelligibility. In simple situations, tradition or common sense notwithstanding, the right thing to do is clear. But many other situations are not at all simple, especially for doctors. A doctor's life-and-death decisions often have enormously complex consequences—for trust between doctor and patient, for pressures felt by old people, and so on. The consequences are so complex, indeed, that they take us right up to the edge of our ability to calculate them to a reliable degree of probability. Doctors need a policy that will both fit a wide range of cases and suitably define a doctor's role in society. Doctors therefore face a dilemma: obvious moral considerations, especially the relief of suffering, impel a doctor to action; complex consequences of such action ramifying through society, many of them damaging, restrain a doctor from action. It is natural that in this dilemma, doctors should look to others for their concurrence, partly because many heads can be better than one, but more importantly because we are all in this together, and, as the issue is so opaque, we should all have a hand in framing the policy to which we may one day be subject. Society will thereby define this part of a doctor's role, and, if it does not do it badly, also define for us what is right and wrong about euthanasia in these highly complex cases. Moral decision here merges with social decision. And here our moral life would be lived out not only in society, but also through it. It may sound unduly conservative to say, as I have said, that, given human nature, our general approach to a value such as life in fixing a policy about killing has to be the modest one of respecting it, not the God-like one of promoting it. But that claim is compatible with a belief that we should work to bring yet more cases—such as euthanasia—under the competing norm, Limit the damage. And it is compatible as well with the belief that we ought to promote life in other ways—say, by helping the starving a good deal more than we do now.

10. *The metaethical standing of these norms*

What forces shape the complex moral standards I have been looking at? The protection of interests is one such force. But there are so many others that we cannot just assume that the metaethical standing of interests will simply be transferred to these complex moral standards.

The norm, Don't deliberately kill the innocent, seems very different from the norm that I looked at earlier, Don't be cruel. Life is a core value, requiring that in some form or other we both respect and promote it. The precise form that the respect and promotion should take, however, needs to be settled, not least because respect and promotion can conflict. The judgement, 'That's cruel', resting as it does on a claim about pain and an agent's intentions, is especially reliable; it is a judgement about a core value and fairly accessible facts about persons. Life, too, is a core value, so there must be a parallel, equally reliable judgement about it. The judgement, 'That's murder', must sometimes also be especially reliable: it will be reliable in a clear case when it rests on a compound claim roughly to the effect that a life has been taken with certain intentions. But the situation is different with norms. Norms have domains, areas of application; the boundaries of their domains are settled not just by the interests at stake, but also by conventions, traditions, and conceptions of the limits of agents. Conventions, traditions, and conceptions of human limits are to some degree arbitrary. Different societies may work with more than trivially different ones, and though they may not be equally beneficial, we will often not be able to tell. And in most societies the domains of norms are continually open to challenge and revision—as is the norm against deliberately killing the innocent in the case of euthanasia. But these judgements are highly risky.

Could the norm, Don't deliberately kill the innocent, be especially reliable? It is not strictly a belief; it is a policy or standard. It has a related belief form: Deliberately killing the innocent is wrong. If we have a plain, paradigmatic case in mind, we should be prepared to say that it is true. It would be virtually the judgement we considered a moment ago, 'That's murder', said in a clear case. But we should have some hesitation about saying that it is true without these restrictions; there are too many exceptions that fit under the related norm, Limit the damage. That just raises again the question of the domain of the norms. And we know that the domain of the norm, Don't deliberately kill the innocent, is not necessarily fixed for ever. Our present policy might, for good reason, change. Policies do not have a truth-value in the plain sense that statements about the natural world do; but they do have a rationale, and so are open to criticism. And norms do not pass the realist's causal test in any satisfactory way. If there is a convergence between us in this standard or policy, it is not best explained in terms of our all coming to recognize how things are in the world. The convergence can be partly explained in those realist terms—namely, in terms of our recognizing certain interests and intentions—but it also has to be explained in terms of the conventions and traditions that have emerged in our society and of the limits to the area of application of the norm that we—though not necessarily all of us—accept.

VIII

HOW CAN WE IMPROVE OUR ETHICAL BELIEFS?

1. *The role of beliefs of high reliability*

How can we improve our ethical beliefs? In pondering that question, we naturally think about how we improve our beliefs in general. And then we inevitably think of the natural sciences: over the last four centuries, no other body of belief has grown as much in range and reliability. In the sciences justification takes a holistic, not a foundationalist, form. No belief stands on its own; all beliefs can be supported, or challenged, by other beliefs. The dominant version of holism is the coherence theory: one justifies beliefs by bringing the set into coherence. In the case of the sciences, the idea of 'coherence' bears a rich interpretation: the beliefs that constitute a science form a systematic unity, a network of credibility transfers that can raise the level of the whole set of beliefs.[1] A theory of justification in the sciences has to find a place for perceptual input from a non-conceptual world; but when it does, it is not clear whether it remains strictly a coherence theory, or becomes a hybrid coherence-foundationalist theory or something else again.[2] But what is important for the purposes of justification is that the beliefs' forming a systematic explanatory whole has a bootstrap effect: there are two-way credibility transfers between the beliefs that, if they become extensive enough, substantially raise the credibility level of the whole.

If we take a natural science as our model for ethics, then our ambition is not the modest one of improving our ethical beliefs where we can, but instead the altogether grander project of justifying ethics itself, of finding sanction or support for the whole set of beliefs. And our way of going about this is likely to be the way that has proved so successful in the sciences: we try to bring our beliefs into coherence or equilibrium.

But there is a problem. Ethics is not like a natural science in what seems to be the key respect. Coherence in science gets its justificatory power from a science's being a systematic, explanatory unification of beliefs. That is what produces the bootstrap effect. The aim of the sciences is to describe the natural world, which we take to be a functional unity.[3] The success of an explanation in one area, therefore, has implications for the success of an explanation in another. There are credibility transfers along these lines of implication, because our beliefs form a system. They form a system because we believe their subject to be a functional unity. Our belief that it is a functional unity is one we start with, but it is also itself supported by the rest of the beliefs in the system. Thus, the success of explanation in any area reinforces that in other areas to which it has inferential connections, and the bootstrap effect occurs. But there is no system of this sort to be found in ethics. Our ethical beliefs, along with various non-ethical beliefs that are relevant to them, can, of course, stand in inferential relations to one another: there is *some* degree of organization to these beliefs, so they display system in *some* sense. But that is well short of saying that these beliefs form a network of credibility transfers that can raise the level of the whole. For instance, our ethical beliefs, on some views, have quite clear forms of organization: according to utilitarians, the principle of utility is supreme, and all other moral principles are subordinate to it; according to some intuitionists, there are several prima-facie duties all on the same level, which must be weighed against one another when they conflict. But for moral beliefs to be organized in this way is not for them to be organized into a network of credibility transfers with a bootstrap effect. And most people's ethical beliefs vary in generality, from beliefs about particular cases to highly general principles. Beliefs about particular cases can illuminate and support more general beliefs, and vice versa. But this too is a fairly weak sort of system. The explanatory circle is too small; and as most major ethical views display these relations of mutual illumination, we have nothing here that will discriminate between them.[4]

The coherence theory of justification says: bring beliefs into coherence. But that says too little. 'Coherence' has many interpretations, ranging from the rich to the meagre. The only feature common to these different requirements of 'coherence' is largely negative: support is not foundationalist, but holistic. Bringing any set of beliefs into coherence is likely to enhance their credibility somewhat. But the crux is, How much? And will it be enough to deserve to be called 'justification'? In ethics, coherence provides a test of uncertain power.

We need to look for the resources available to us to criticize *ethical* beliefs in particular. The fact that we cannot depend upon a strong bootstrap effect in ethics shifts our attention to beliefs of high reliability. Are there any? How many? And how central are they to our ethical life?

There *are* beliefs of fairly high reliability. One kind are beliefs about interests. There is a particularly solid core of interests: interests that are part of the setting only within which our language is possible. To the core we can then hope to add at least some of the interests constituting what I earlier called the profile of prudential values. How many we can add will depend, of course, on how reliable we think our identification of the values is.[5]

Another kind are certain basic moral beliefs, ones that arise from the core interests, and are almost as deeply embedded in our language as they are. One of the criteria for a 'pain' is its being the sort of thing that we want to avoid or to have alleviated—in short, that it is a disvalue. There are values at stake in my life, some of which I must see as at stake in yours if I am to see you too as a human being. *That it hurts* gives me a reason to avoid it; it also gives me a reason, of some strength, not to do it to you. The engine of those two judgements is *that it hurts*. Whether it is my pain or yours is not part of what carries the judgements. And that line of thought leads to the moral judgements 'That's cruel' and, in certain circumstances, 'I ought to help you'.[6]

A third kind are certain factual beliefs. There are limits to the human will; some forms of impartiality are beyond our reach. There are limits to human knowledge; on some matters we cannot even decide probabilities reliable enough for action. There are natural obstacles to our arriving at beneficial forms of co-operation; if there is to be co-operation on any fairly large social scale, we have to find ways to overcome them.

Not every belief that falls into these three categories is of high reliability; nor of equally high reliability. But why think, in the first place, that any are of *high* reliability? It is hard not to accept that the core values and the basic moral judgements close to them are especially reliable. It is hard not to accept that factual beliefs are too, provided that evidence establishes them fairly securely to be fact. There is some doubt, however, about prudential values out-side the core. I suggested earlier that we have a sensitivity to something's being prudentially valuable, and that there are cri-teria for the sensitivity's succeeding or failing.[7] In the case of some kinds of prudential value, it may prove hard ever to settle whether the criteria for its successful working are met. More investigation of prudential deliberation will have to take place before we shall know how secure our beliefs about certain prudential values are—especially whether, in the right circumstances, convergence in belief actually occurs. It is a reasonable hope, though, that we can add at least some further judgements about prudential values to the set of especially reliable beliefs.

How central to ethics are these beliefs? How much might they contribute to the job of improving our ethical beliefs? Well, inter-ests are certainly central to our seeing an issue as a moral one. There are all sorts of possible links between morality and inter-ests, from the strong utilitarian one to the weak one that I pro-posed in the previous chapter. But there must, I believe, be *some* link between the two.[8] Our ancestors often singled out acts—certain sexual ones are a good example—that harmed no interests, and, by investing them with a certain formal status (for example, forbidden by God), turned them into moral matters. This may seem to show that formal status alone is sufficient to make an issue moral, and that a link to interests cannot therefore be, as I think, necessary. Ethics can certainly be shaped by metaphysics. If we see our lives within a metaphysical framework that includes a good God legislating for us, then a norm's having the status of being God's command is quite enough to make it moral. But that is because we think that God's actions aim at the good. So a link with interests is present even here. God's actions could not be seen as 'good' or 'moral' without their having due regard to in-terests. There is no reason to expect the words 'ethical' and 'moral', any more than most other words in the language, to have a set of essential properties, or even a single necessary condition such as a link to interests. There is no sharp divide between morality on the one side and, say, codes of honour, the standards of a 'lady' or a 'gentleman', and the rules of etiquette on the other.

In any case, I have been speaking so far only of our current conception of morality. The history of ethics is a history of succes-sive extensions of the boundaries of concern—from family to community, from community to humanity, from humanity to animals.[9] What is now being attempted is a further extension to the environment. Will environmental ethics always see itself as constrained to find a link to someone's interests? Our obligations to individual animals, as bearers of interests, tell us nothing about the respect that we may owe to their species—or, in general, to the environment. Environmental ethics is itself in its infancy, and may develop in either of two ways. We may be able to develop it by developing the resources of an already established ethical tradition. Or we may find that the problems it presents are so discontinuous with the concerns that shaped older ethics that we must develop quite new concepts, which would then have in some way to be tied in with our old ones. There have been distinguished attempts to follow the first course,[10] but my guess is that in the end we shall have to follow the second. I suspect that we should see environmental ethics as a search for responses that are 'fitting' or 'appropriate'. There are things in the environment—a virgin forest, say, or the ecosystem of a coral reef—to which the appropriate response is awe or wonder, and the appropriate behaviour is the behaviour that awe and wonder prompt. That there need be no interests at stake does not mean that there are no appropriate or inappropriate actions. It is probably better to speak, though, in terms of appropriate and inappropriate actions rather than in terms of forests' having 'rights' and humans' having 'duties' to them. Because the boundaries are unavoidably fuzzy, it is not worth debating whether environmental ethics, on the conception of it that I favour, is really part of 'morality'. Anything that one says about morality is vulnerable to a sufficiently radical shift in conception of what 'morality' is. Still, the possibility that one has not told the whole story about a future, extended morality does not mean that one would want to tell differently the story that one tells about it now, on our current conception. And on our current conception, morality has a link with interests. So one of the categories of beliefs of high reliability—namely, interests—is certainly central to morality.

This centrality might hold out prospects of comprehensiveness, though not yet much power, in criticizing ethics. The link between morality and interests can take many different forms, and we need a way to rule out some of them. Here another category of beliefs of high reliability can play a role. There are facts about agents and about societies. They give rise to constraints upon moral norms. For instance, one cannot adopt certain highly indirect forms of utilitarianism if they put at the centre of moral thought forms of reasoning that are beyond our capacity. If my line of thought in the previous chapter was sound, the constraints that one can derive from facts about agents and society lead to a morality different from familiar forms of consequentialism, deontology, and virtue ethics. They suggest a morality with certain similarities to the law. According to it, the live issue about the norm, Don't deliberately kill the innocent, is its boundaries. Can we make an exception for euthanasia? For abortion? We see, at least in rough outline, how to go about answering those questions. We have to decide whether there is a clear enough case for a new policy on euthanasia, say, manageable by the likes of us, with all our limitations, in the kind of society in which we would have to operate it. In general, beliefs of high reliability provide constraints on ethics. Some are constraints of intelligibility (the accommodation of those values that are part of the framework without which language would be impossible). But these constraints rule out only the most implausible ethical outlooks, leaving many still in contest. There are also constraints of feasibility (what is feasible, given what a good life is like, what agents are like, and what societies are like). These are the constraints that hold promise of greater critical powers.

2. Stages in criticizing ethics

The criticism of ethics can be looked upon as occurring in two stages. The first consists in forming a picture of what goes on in making judgements about prudential values and moral norms. It is the work that I have tried to do in the case of prudential values in Chapters II–IV and in the case of moral norms in Chapters V–VII. It cannot, in the end, be done without adopting substantive views about what a good life is like and what moral standards there are. So it involves deciding upon a general moral view: utilitarianism, deontology, virtue ethics, my own account, or whatever. I started this book with questions that anyone, regardless of ethical outlook, had to face. The book looked like being a prolegomenon to *any* ethics. It was to be about our critical techniques.

And are critical techniques not neutral as to subject-matter? But it has ended up with my adopting one particular ethical view, and rejecting others, and having to do this in order to explain at all fully our critical powers in ethics. This progression from neutrality to commitment seems to me inevitable. One cannot carry one's critical thoughts very far without some idea of what the genesis, point, and content of the subject is. And arriving at that idea already involves the exercise of some critical powers.

The second stage is this. The picture formed at the first stage will then tell us how to judge claims about particular prudential values and moral norms. The picture shows us what prudential and moral judgements aim at being. For instance, it shows something about the origin and ground of norms by plotting their connection to the various forces that shape them: interests, facts about agents and society, and so on. Having once plotted these connections, we can see how generally to go about assessing the norms.

Can we reasonably hope to carry out the first stage? Well, facts about the limits of knowledge and of the will are hardly easy to establish. For one thing, they are a complex mix of the empirical and the normative. Judgements about the limits of the will, for example, involve judgements about what a prudentially good life is like and how the commitments that it involves affect the will. And even if the facts about these limits were themselves highly reliable, the important derivations we make from them, in using them as constraints of feasibility on the contents of ethics, are distinctly shaky. That the most plausible forms of consequentialism are the least feasible ones is not itself a judgement that one could class as highly reliable. But what it suggests is not that the work of the sort attempted in Chapters II–IV and especially in Chapters V–VII cannot be carried out, but that it yields conclusions around which uncertainty is bound to linger. Carrying out the work of the first stage, unlike bringing one's scientific beliefs into coherence, is not a progression toward increasingly secure or justified beliefs.

How do we carry out the second stage? There does not seem to be any one method involved. The work of the second stage is much more piecemeal than that. Once we have a picture of the connections between norms and the forces that shape them—interests, facts about agents, facts about society—then the most effective way for us to give support to a particular norm is by showing that it stands in the right sort of relation to interests or to facts about agents or to the successful working of society. Arguments to this effect are likely to follow a different pattern from case to case.

For example, we do not in any proper sense 'justify' such a conceptually basic norm as 'Don't be cruel'. It raises no questions about the limits of the will or of knowledge. It seems to be a limiting case: it marks the point where justification more or less comes to an end. All that one can do to support the judgement 'That would be cruel' is to lay bare the conceptual links between the notions 'cruel' and 'pain', and between 'pain' and what we wish to avoid or have alleviated.[11] But these notions are all so close to the ground floor that it is hard to regard any one of them as justification for the other.

The norm 'Don't deliberately kill the innocent' requires quite different treatment. In a way, it too needs no justification: the value of life, like freedom from pain, is too central to our recognition of someone as a human being for there to be room for justification. The live issue, however, is precisely what the boundaries of the norm are, and here the limitations of agents do matter. Agents like us must in general live by the norm, Don't deliberately kill the innocent. But in some cases we follow the norm, Limit the damage. The live issue is whether the sorts of cases now widely thought to fall under the first norm, such as euthanasia, might better be placed under the second. In some particularly simple cases, it may be obvious that euthanasia is the right thing. But in more complicated cases—say, cases in which what is at issue is a public policy that will be applied fairly widely—the central question will be whether there is any formulation of it that can be applied by the likes of us and still serve the aim of limiting the damage. That is an enormously complicated question, not just about values, but also about agents, society, and, importantly, how agents in a society should jointly take a difficult decision that might end up seriously affecting any one of them.

3. *The idea of 'justifying' ethics*

'Coherence' is a theory of justification. But does ethics lend itself to 'justification'? Is there some overall structure into which we can put our ethical (and related) beliefs—a foundationalist, linear structure or a coherentist, spherical structure or some yet undescribed structure—which will endorse them as sound? I have mentioned various, rather heterogeneous ways in which one might hope to criticize and improve one's ethical beliefs; but no overall justifying structure, no overarching system of credibility transfers appropriate to ethics, is likely to emerge from them. Making one's ethical (and related) beliefs coherent is indeed likely to improve them a bit; but what seems to be missing is any reason to think that it will so transform them that, at some ideal limit, they will become sound.

We philosophers have two quite different, incompatible conceptions of the relation of philosophy to ethics. First, as philosophers, we assert hegemony over ethics. We think of ethics as a branch of philosophy. We say that one cannot 'do ethics' unless one is prepared to 'do philosophy'. Of course, non-philosophers have views about ethics; they announce, criticize, and amend ethical principles, but to the extent that they do any of this properly, they have in effect to become philosophers. Ethics exists, of course, independently of philosophy, but philosophy's job is to come on the scene and reconstruct this body of unreliable, common-sense beliefs into a much firmer structure, by testing beliefs, purging the weak and retaining the strong. Philosophy's transforming task is to justify, sanction, and, if possible, systematize.

But we philosophers have, as well, an altogether more modest conception. We admit that a subtle, complex, deep ethics exists quite independently of philosophy. Long before philosophy came on the scene, societies had solved any number of co-operation problems, and worked out a serviceable picture of the limits of the human will and knowledge. These solutions and these pictures are, to make no stronger claim, not markedly worse than what philosophers now come up with. When philosophers arrive on the scene, they can criticize and suggest changes to prevailing ethical beliefs. But then, so can non-philosophers, and if what is central to successful criticism is a shrewd sense of how to live well and of how people and societies work, then it is not clear what special standing philosophers can claim in this work. So philosophers ought to be sceptical both about how great anyone's powers of criticism in ethics can be and about how great a philosopher's particular contribution to the task can be.

It is surprising that the first, ambitious conception still has so much life in it. But philosophers still commonly speak of ethical views as 'theories'. And talk of 'theories' makes it easier to think of ethics as being explanatory and potentially systematic—that is, much like a natural science. And that would explain why one might think that bringing one's ethical beliefs into coherence would be a form of 'justification'.

But our moral norms seem to arise in different ways to meet different needs, without any overarching background considera-tion, either substantive or formal, generating and sanctioning them. The aim of ethics is to provide norms for us to live by, not to provide the sort of system of beliefs that would lend itself to any known form of justification. If one sees one's moral outlook as an assemblage of norms arrived at in a piecemeal fashion, then one is much less likely to call it a 'theory'. We can criticize and im-prove certain of our norms, but to improve here and there is not to justify overall. Justification, in the strong sense that we are accustomed to, is not a project suited to ethics. We are reluctant to accept that, because we are still to some degree under the sway of the Cartesian dichotomy: a belief is either justified, or it is a prejudice. But we start with the norms of those who have gone before us. We demand of these norms that they be serviceable protections of values, and some of them fairly obviously are. The norm, Don't deliberately kill the innocent, protects the value of life, and it, along with related norms such as, Limit the damage, pass any reasonable test of serviceability. And we constantly sub-ject them to criticism, which sometimes results in amendment. That is enough to undermine the dichotomy: justified or a prejudice.

4. The stuff of reflection

There are beliefs of high reliability—beliefs about interests, about certain basic moral matters, about certain features of agents and society. We can bring these various elements together in a single, rather rough picture of forms of a basic good life for the likes of us living, as we do, in large societies in modern conditions. It was this picture that began, in the previous chapter, to eliminate possible accounts of moral norms—for instance, familiar forms of utilitarianism, deontology, and virtue ethics. And it is this norm-atively and empirically complex picture, I think, that will help most in our critical reflection on ethics.

Modern moral philosophy, it has often been observed,[12] has tried to work with a much sparer picture. It has embarked, rightly I think, on the project of developing a secular ethics. It was right if only because religious belief yields no more than a few highly indeterminate moral precepts, leaving it to us, religious believers or not, to fill in the rest from other sources. Ethics is, of necessity, a largely secular concern. So modern moral philosophy cleared the ground of God, divine commandments, and the hierarchical social order that coexisted with religion in Europe (even if it coexisted oddly with the egalitarian elements in Christian teach-ing) before the rise of robust forms of individualism in the seven-teenth and eighteenth centuries. It then tried to locate ethics on the largely featureless terrain that was left. It sought the source of moral standards, instead, in each individual. The only figures in its landscape were individual agents, whom it endowed with no more than rationality and a psychologically rather simple capacity for happiness and unhappiness. In the utilitarian programme, an individual agent needed for the purpose only a maximizing prin-ciple and powers of calculation. In the Kantian programme, the individual needed only a fairly elementary knowledge of human nature and a capacity to detect contradiction. It is not surprising that, when it came to choosing between these spare modern con-ceptions, an equally spare test was thought to be adequate—merely one more exercise of our logical powers, a coherence test.

But it has become clear to many that ethics is not possible in such spare surroundings. Our job now is to make agents much more lifelike. We need to develop our substantive views about human well-being. Modern philosophy had largely abandoned that project. It is not that it ignored it entirely; it merely did not think that it needed it. A simple hedonism was widely accepted, espe-cially in British philosophy, to be succeeded eventually by what was intended as a neutral preference account of value.[13] What remained constant in this tradition throughout its development was an adherence to the taste model of prudential values.[14] We have only just begun to work out a more adequate model. There is no reason to think that, in the course of doing this, we may make 'discoveries' the departure of which from common sense will be of revolutionary proportions. What is needed is more a matter of focusing what we know than of discovering what we do not know. Still, we do not yet have even the most basic vocabulary for talking about prudential values; in Chapter II I had to invent most of the names I gave them. We must now work out and adopt some such vocabulary, to give agents their major commitments and aspirations. We must give them their incapacities as well as their capacities; we need to learn much more about the limits of the will, and how those limits are affected by what well-being turns out to be. We must give agents autonomy, and accept the consequent clashes between them over what makes life good. We must make our surroundings, too, much more lifelike. We must accommodate society's great size and its lack of personal ties. We must identify efficient means of production, the demands they make on co-operation, and the problems they create for the distribution of rewards. Games theory is a significant start, but it leaves many important questions unaddressed: for example, How unbendable do social rules need to be? How simple and firm should dispositions be?

I have said that we must make agents more lifelike. But how much more? If we describe them in great detail, we shall lose the distance, the abstraction, needed for rational criticism. The spare conception of agents that I am objecting to is part of what is now called modernism: the world picture that emerged from the seventeenth century's scientific revolution and the eighteenth century's optimistic rationalism. The major project now facing critics of modernism is to determine how much more lifelike the conception must be, to decide what balance to strike between the concrete and the abstract, the embedded and the detached. That the internal argument among critics of modernism has gone on for so long is because we lack a convincing, reasoned answer to the question, How much more? In ethics, we can answer that question, I think, by describing the role that moral norms play in our lives, and in particular how norms arise and take the shape they do. That story requires drawing on features of agents and society that go well beyond the spare individual of modernism, but still retain a degree of abstraction. It is the story started, though not finished, in the last six chapters, and it centres on *human* capacities and incapacities and what it is for *human* life to flourish in a *modern society*.

In offering a list of beliefs of high reliability, I purport to be offering materials that will substantially help in refining our ethical thought. How far will this refinement go? One form of scepticism about any refinement of ethics is that the critical resources available to us outside any single moral view are either suspect or so thin as not to get us very far, while the critical resources available inside any one moral view may serve to amend that view here and there, but are too embedded in one way of looking at the world to be able to adjudicate between very different ones. There is, of course, no denying the problem: how far outside one's own particular way of looking at the world, how free of the quite detailed interpretative and critical concepts that have evolved in one's own culture or one's own group within it, can one get? But that is not a problem, I think, to be accepted on its own terms. It speaks of thick concepts deeply embedded in one people's way of making sense of their experience and of a point outside so thinly described that its authority, especially as an Archimedean point for ethics, is suspect. It speaks of an 'inside' and an 'outside'. But that is a false dichotomy. The most important fact about our critical vocabulary for ethics is that so much has still to be developed. We have concepts too thick to serve, and others—the conceptual equipment of the spare individual agent of modern moral philosophy—too thin to serve. Our critical vocabulary will consist of the key terms in a successful account of human well-being, not yet settled, and in its related picture of realistically drawn agents living satisfactory lives in a realistically drawn society, also not yet settled. Again, I doubt that the critical vocabulary will turn out to be revolutionary (ideas such as 'accomplishment' and 'understanding' take much work to define and name interests that have a real existence independent of our actual motivation and language, but they are unlikely in the end to astonish us). Still, the language of prudential values is not now readily accessible.

Once this critical vocabulary has been developed and we look back at our original conceptual framework and ask whether we are inside or outside it, I think we are likely to drop the question as ill drawn. We shall have substantially expanded our original conceptual framework; it seems enough to say that. There is no quick way to see why, and where, we should position ourselves between those who are confident of our ability to justify the whole body of ethical belief and those who doubt that we can make any significant critical headway. But the previous six chapters have provided one answer to those questions.

Our first real critical task is to compose, out of what we have in the way of beliefs of high reliability, a picture of what it is for a human agent to live a good life among other agents, many of them strangers, doing the same. This picture should be the pivot of our thought in ethics. It leaves space for all the plausible general moral views to make their case, while the picture itself sets the basic terms for the debate between them. This takes us back to the spare landscape in which modern moral philosophers have sought to cultivate ethics. It will not grow there. One of our chief tasks now is to find the ground on which it will grow and to move it there.

NOTES

CHAPTER I

1. The case against piecemeal appeal to intuition has been made power-fully by others, particularly by R. M. Hare and R. B. Brandt. See Hare, 'The Argument from Received Opinion', in Hare 1971; also Hare 1981: ch. 8. See Brandt 1979: ch. 1. See also Singer 1974.

2. On, e.g. psychological causes, see Freud 1957: 138: 'Ethics must be regarded . . . as a therapeutic effort: as an endeavour to achieve some-thing through the standards imposed by the super-ego which had not been attained by the work of civilization in other ways. We already know—it is what we have been discussing—that the question is how to dislodge the greatest obstacle to civilization, the constitutional tendency in men to aggressions against one another.' Freud ought to have inserted 'in part' between 'regarded' and 'as a therapeutic ef-fort'. But he must have identified here an important cause of why one person inclines to one set of moral views and another to a dif-ferent set. I myself suspect that we often find, through the workings of a mechanism of compensation, an overly strict super-ego associ-ated with relatively unstrict moral intuitions, and vice versa. But the moral views of any reflective person will be shaped by vastly more sorts of causes than just the ones that Freud mentions. For an exam-ple of such psychological speculation, see Westermarck 1932: chs. 8 and 9.

3. In Old English 'ought' was the past tense of the verb 'to owe', and was used in that way until quite recently (e.g. by Shakespeare). 'Should' comes from a Teutonic root meaning 'to owe', and in Middle English there was a transitive use of 'shall' and 'should' meaning 'to owe'. A 'duty' is what is owed, from the Latin *debere*, a sense it still retains in customs halls. 'Merit' comes from the Latin *meritum*, meaning 'price', 'value', 'service rendered'. To 'retribute' is to repay. To 'oblige' is to bind or to make indebted. And so on.

   Still, etymology is not meaning, and all of these words, despite their origins, have taken on a life of their own. But their origin still makes itself felt; we still talk, as if it were a far more decisive move in an argument than it is, of *paying one's debt* to society, of not *owing* anything to nations of the Third World, and so on.

4. Quine 1953: 91 ff. On intuition in the natural sciences, see e.g. Newton-Smith 1981: 197, 212–13. On intuition in philosophy see e.g.

Nozick 1981: 546; Rorty 1980: 34. We find what seems to me the right sort of ambivalence about intuitions, the right mixture of scepticism and respect, much more commonly in these other departments of thought. On the side of respect, see Jaako Hintikka's introduction to Hintikka 1967: 3: 'An intriguing aspect of the completeness and incompleteness results is that one of their starting-points (viz. our concept of what constitutes completeness) is inevitably an idea which can perhaps be formulated in naïve set-theoretic terms but which either is not formulated axiomatically to begin with or which (in the case of incompleteness) cannot even possibly be so formulated. Yet concepts of this kind are most interesting. We seem to have many clear intuitions concerning them, and it is important to develop ways of handling them.' On the side of scepticism, see Daniel Dennett's and Douglas Hofstadter's complaint about the 'intuition pump', the use of one sort of example to push our intuitions in a particular direction (say, in a debate about whether computers think), in Hofstadter and Dennett 1982: 375, 459.

5. Kant 1961: esp. sect. 2. I explain my views on Kant's categorical imperative and its ethical content somewhat more fully in Griffin 1986: Ch. X, sect. 4. For a corrective to this common but over-simplified reading of Kant, see e.g. O'Neill 1989; Herman 1993.

6. Hare hopes to derive ethical principles entirely from the semantics of key moral terms—not local, culture-bound terms like 'chastity' or 'humility', but global ones like 'good' and 'ought'. See Hare 1952: ch. 11; Hare 1963: chs. 2, 3, 6, 7; and Hare 1981: chs. 1, 2.5, 4.1 ff. Global terms define what we all think of as morality, and therefore any feature essential to them, it would seem, must be accepted by anyone who accepts the authority of morality. One feature that Hare finds is that judgements made with 'good' and 'ought' must be universalizable, in the relatively weak sense that we be able to purge those judgements of reference to particular persons, times, or places. But this seems to be an escapable requirement. Even if (as I think) Hare is right that such judgements must be universalizable, universalizability is a requirement only if one uses those key terms as they are used now. One might, however, see reason to use them slightly differently in a way that would threaten universalizability. The same is possible if, to universalizability, one adds further features that one thinks essential to key moral terms—for instance, as Hare would propose, prescriptivity. Prescriptivity is escapable in the same way. And prescriptivity is not, in any case, very powerful in its effects. Prescriptivity and universalizability can jointly turn into a strong test of moral right and wrong of the sort that Kant's categorical imperative is, but only if they are filled out in the context of a fairly rich account of

rationality, rich enough to embody judgements about what moral reasons are good reasons. All that can be derived from the semantics of the key terms is a fairly weak, schematic notion of impartiality—entirely neutral, for instance, between the ideal observer interpretation of impartiality in utilitarianism and the ideal contractor interpretation in modern contractualism. In order to get much in the way of interesting substantive moral conclusions out of the notion of impartiality, we have to build more content into it. It is true that formal features, such as universalizability and prescriptivity, impose *some* limits on what can count as a moral judgement. We cannot change the formal features of moral terms too drastically before we find that we have ended up with a vocabulary with which we can no longer make what we now understand as a 'moral' judgement. But that is not a severe limitation. The questions that we ask now may not be quite the right ones. And the interesting moral features, such as universalizability, though (as I should myself say) present now in key moral terms, are the sort that could easily be much modified with further understanding. I doubt that they will be; but that belief rests on my beliefs about substantive morality: I think that in working morality out we shall not come upon sufficient reasons to drop, say, universalizability from the key moral terms. Still, in developing ethics, all concepts are up for revision. It is just that our decisions about the concepts depend in part on our decisions about substantive views in ethics. So we have, not a linear derivation from an independently justified starting-point in semantics, but a more holistic justification with one part resting on others which eventually, perhaps through intermediaries, rest also on it. And the question will therefore obviously arise, Do intuitions creep back in to provide us with the substantive views we use?

Now, Hare is well aware that his view is open to the charge of linguistic conservatism. See Hare 1981: ch. 1.5; for further discussion, see J. L. Mackie's objections in Mackie 1984 and Hare's reply in Hare 1984*a*. His claim is that from the universal prescriptivity of moral judgements we can derive a form of impartiality, broadly utilitarian, that would determine which principles and dispositions should guide action. To the charge that he is making us the captive of our present conceptual scheme, Hare replies that he would be if he concentrated on what he calls 'secondarily evaluative words', like 'chaste' and 'humble', but that he concentrates instead on words like 'must' and 'ought', which encapsulate a commitment only to morality itself, not to any particular morality. But the real worry, I have been suggesting, is different from the one he here meets: namely, that even 'ought' and 'must' encapsulate particular commitments as to what morality, or moral reasoning, is. Hare's answer to this deeper worry is, I believe, that if we alter the meanings of the most basic evaluative words, we shall alter the questions we ask, and that if we want to answer *those* questions, then we are stuck with *those* concepts. But the worry persists. We might, in the course of building any theory, revise certain features of its key terms, so that we should no longer be asking exactly the same questions as at the start, or entirely new ones either. Could there be, initially, any ground for saying that such partial revision will not, or should not, take place? Pressures to change concepts usually mount only in the course of searching for an adequate moral point of view. So can one do more than search, always sensitive to the option of conceptual innovation? This, of course, allows Hare a further response—in fact, the one with which I expressed sympathy. He can say that when the search is over we will have found no need to revise the universal prescriptivity of 'ought' and 'must'. But this can be said only when we already have the content of our moral beliefs; universal prescriptivity cannot be its source. So again, we are left wondering whether purism is a live option.

7. The key moral terms of ordinary language are, Brandt thinks, too vague as they stand to allow definite results. See Brandt 1979: ch. 1 and Brandt 1985. His solution is for us to adopt a more normative approach—namely, *reforming* definitions. Pre-empt the term 'rational', he suggests, for 'survives maximal criticism by facts and logic'. For our traditional question, 'What is morally right?', substitute, 'What is allowed by any moral code that rational persons would want for a society in which they were to spend their lives?' (Brandt 1979: 193–4). This reforming definition gives the traditional question a clearer, more manageable sense by making it empirical: namely, a question of fact about what people desire in certain circumstances. The term 'rational' here is to be thought of as entirely free of value judgements (ibid. 13). No appeal to moral intuitions is therefore needed.

There seem to me to be two problems with Brandt's sort of purism. How do we decide which is the best reforming definition? There are altogether too many shapes that a reforming definition might take. Why not, instead of Brandt's, adopt the definition, What personal moral code would I, if I were rational, choose to live by in the light of what others are most likely to do? And this is only one of very many different, attractive alternatives, which to some degree run parallel to the very large variety of forms that indirect utilitarianism can take. My worry is, How do we choose between them? Brandt is aware that we are not restricted to only one question (ibid. 185), but my worry remains. If I both get my desires rational and free myself from logical error, it is likely that I shall still be left wondering which of many remaining reforming definitions to choose. Would there be any resort left to me then but to appeal to substantive moral beliefs?

And, anyway, why confine my search for reforming definitions to ones that are entirely empirical? I think that most of us would agree with Brandt that no *unsupported* value judgements should appear in reforming definitions; otherwise the whole project of finding a justification for moral beliefs is undermined. And most of us would also agree that appeal to unsifted intuitions does not provide adequate support. But why think that there is no better support for a normative judgement than that? It is true that the appearance of a value judgement in a reforming definition might just introduce a personal prejudice of the person offering the definition. No doubt value judgements often do just that. But it is a large assumption, and a question-begging one, to hold that all do. It is to assume that there are no objective moral reasons for action, recognizable as such. But this is to assume answers to most of the large metaethical questions about the nature of values and the possibilities of knowledge of them. So Brandt's method of reforming definitions is not self-standing; it rests on answers to those large epistemological and metaphysical questions.

So the two problems about Brandt's purist view are, I think, these: first, it is far from clear that the method can be fully carried out without appeal to substantive moral beliefs somewhere along the way, and, second, the plausibility of the method comes entirely from answers to metaethical questions that we have not yet been given any reason to accept.

8. See Chs. II–IV.

9. This is what Anthony Giddens has called the 'double hermeneutic' feature of the human sciences; see Giddens 1977: 12 and Giddens 1993: introduction to 2nd edn. and conclusion. I am indebted to John Tasioulas for discussion on this topic.

10. See Wittgenstein 1953: *passim*, but esp. sects. 1–38, 136–56, 167–238; 1967: sects. 338–91. For references to 'form of life', see 1953: sects. 19, 23, 241; 1969: sects. 358–9, 559.

11. See e.g. Donald Davidson, 'Psychology as Philosophy', p. 237, and 'Mental Events', p. 222, both in Davidson 1980; also his Lindley Lecture (1982). I slur over here the differences between Wittgenstein and Davidson. Wittgenstein's notion of a 'form of life' seems to give place to local practices as well as to universal human features. Davidson's truth-condition semantics locates meaning in the match between sentences and their truth conditions, and the structure of the match between my sentences and some stranger's sentences can occur independently of local practices.

12. See e.g. Lakatos 1963–4. See also Michael Dummett's argument against

the law of excluded middle and in favour of an intuitionist mathematics; for a recent statement of the issue see Dummett 1991: 9–11. See also the discussion of these matters in Newton-Smith 1981.

13. John Rawls is its most influential proponent. See Rawls 1972: sects. 4 and 9. See also Rawls 1951; Rawls 1974–5: esp. sect. 2; Rawls 1980.

14. A point made by Susan Haack in her 1993: 25–6.

15. Hempel 1967: 83.

16. e.g. Bonjour 1985: 99.

17. This, I say, is the now dominant interpretation of 'coherence'. But hardly just now: see Bradley 1914: 210; Blanshard 1939: ii. 275–6.

18. This well-known objection goes back at least to Russell 1906–7.

19. See Bonjour 1985: 107.

20. Whether, in light of the underdetermination of theory by observation, our accommodating perceptual input will, on its own, ensure that we arrive at a *unique* set may be doubted; but whatever one thinks about the matter of underdetermination, that is not a complication that bothers just coherence theories. See Dancy 1985: 114–16.

21. As the following believe: Bonjour 1985: 112–19; Lehrer 1990: 145–6 (though, Lehrer adds, with 'elements of foundationalism'); and in the domain of ethics Brink 1989: 135–9.

22. As Haack 1993: 19 claims.

23. The same conclusion holds if, instead of considering the conditions for the intelligibility of language generally, we consider those, more specifically, of *ethical* language. For me to see your concerns as ethical, I have to see them as giving human and animal interests a fairly central place, showing respect of some sort for others, and so on. But these constraints rule out only pretty odd views; the views that we seriously wonder about and try to choose between are still left in contention. I say more about the concept of the ethical in Ch. VIII, sect. 1.

24. For a good discussion of these issues, see Hurley 1989.

25. I have John Rawls particularly in mind. For his definition of 'considered judgements', see Rawls 1972: 47–8; see also p. 20.

26. Rawls's criteria for 'considered' judgements would often leave one with pretty dubious beliefs. Why confine ourselves to intuitions of which we are relatively *confident*? Confidence in ethics has different psychological explanations, many of them not reassuring. The confident ethical beliefs of a thoroughly comfortable member of a privileged class might be his worst; his best might be his occasional unconfident glimmerings of a different way of life. And why confine ourselves to *calm* judgements? Many people's best moral thinking is reserved for their deathbed or their doctor's waiting-room (a point made by Daniels 1979: 258). Etc. Anyway, to say that we should interest

ourselves only in judgements formed in the absence of conditions likely to corrupt judgement begs the important questions. If we knew which conditions did that, and also knew that we were avoiding them, we should indeed be able to isolate a class of especially reliable judgements. But we do not know it.

27. See Chs. II–IV.

28. See Chs. V–VII.

29. In any case, I have my doubts about the first sort of system; see Ch. VII.

30. This yields what Rawls calls 'wide reflective equilibrium': 'There are several interpretations of reflective equilibrium. For the notion varies depending upon whether one is to be presented with only those descriptions which more or less match one's existing judgements except for minor discrepancies, or whether one is to be presented with all possible descriptions to which one might plausibly conform one's judgements together with all relevant philosophical arguments for them [i.e. wide reflective equilibrium]' (Rawls 1972: 49).

31. See Ch. IV, sect. 2.

32. It is true that we should not need to look for highly reliable *ethical* beliefs if we could assess competing moral views just by appealing to non-moral matters of fact. All we should then have to do is to find the relevant, highly reliable, factual beliefs. And facts about human motivation and about how societies work go a long way toward weeding out unrealistic moral views. This possibility raises a raft of familiar questions about the relation of fact and value, particularly about reductive naturalism—the view that ethical beliefs can be reduced to factual ones, on roughly Hume's understanding of the 'factual'. I find reductive naturalism implausible (see Ch. III). But the facts that do indeed go a long way toward testing moral views (e.g. facts about human motivation and about how societies work) are far from purely factual. For instance, some moral views rest on dubious conceptions of the human will. But we cannot determine the limits of the will independently of knowing what are plausible human goals and how inspiring they are. The capacity of the will is partly a function of its goals. So any 'fact' likely to get far in testing competing moral views will be partly constituted by beliefs about values; we shall not know whether it is highly reliable without knowing whether its constituent ethical beliefs are too.

33. I suggest: there can be no test of much strength for normative ethics without answers to certain key metaethical questions. The most prominent proponent of the coherence theory in our time is John Rawls, and his special contribution to it has been to maintain: the test for ethical beliefs is largely independent of metaethics.

His reason is this. Metaethics is concerned with such questions as whether and in what sense moral judgements are true, whether they are objective, whether values form an order independent of human belief and attitude, when they can be known, and so on (see Rawls 1972: 51 ff.; Rawls 1974–5: 5–7; Rawls 1980: 554). Normative ethics, by contrast, is the systematic, comparative study of competing general moral views—utilitarianism, Kantianism, virtue theory, and so on. The programme of normative ethics is to develop each view, probably much further than they have yet been developed, then to compare their features, and also importantly, on that basis, to decide on their relative adequacy (see Rawls 1974–5: 8). For my own part, I decide their adequacy by bringing my own beliefs into wide coherence. Once the rest of you have also done this with your beliefs, we may find ourselves converging on some of the same beliefs. If enough of us converge, then we may be willing to regard the beliefs converged upon as objective (see Rawls 1974–5: 9; Rawls 1980: 554, 570). And we might then also be in a position to settle issues about the truth of moral judgements, the independent reality of values, and other metaethical difficulties as well (see Rawls 1980: 564–5). In this way, Rawls argues not just for the independence of normative ethics from metaethics (see Rawls 1974–5: 9, 21), but also for its priority (see Rawls 1972: 53; Rawls 1974–5: 6, 21). At this stage in the history of philosophy, he says, we are not in a position to make much headway with metaethics; but we have just seen ways in which, with advance in normative ethics, we might eventually make advance in metaethics too.

But can we describe a test powerful enough to rank competing normative views, while ignoring mataethical questions about objectivity, truth, or knowledge? The test at work in normative ethics must yield a ranking in a strong sense. It must lead us not merely to a preference between the competing views, but to a decision as to which has more reason on its side. It must guard against the quite ordinary ways in which our moral beliefs go wrong. It must meet doubts about our beliefs that arise from our own past mistakes—that is, not extreme philosophical doubts about whether we can know anything, or at least anything about values, which is a problem that we consign to metaethics, but entirely realistic doubts. Rawls agrees (see Rawls 1972: 50, 53, 121, 452; Rawls 1974–5: 8–9; Rawls 1980: 534, 568–9). In describing the ranking, he regularly uses terms that carry considerable epistemic weight. We compare moral views, he says at one point, on the basis of, among other things, how well they accommodate facts about the human psyche and society; that decides what Rawls calls their 'feasibility'. Then, given their feasibility, we look at their content in wide coherence; that decides their 'reasonableness' (Rawls 1974–5: 15; Rawls 1980: 534). And, for Rawls, decisions about reasonableness have to come largely from each individual's reaching wide coherence; the further step of convergence between different individuals' beliefs adds little. Lack of convergence can, it is true, serve as a trip-wire. My lack of convergence with the rest of you on what I claim to see trips up my claim to see, but whatever special reliability reports of perception have rests primarily, not on convergence, but on what individual perception is. Similarly, convergence between you and me in ethics matters to the justification of belief only if it is what has been called 'principled' convergence—that is, convergence arising from your or my having separately applied standards of reasonableness to the formation of our own beliefs. Rawls agrees with this too (Rawls 1974–5: 9).

But his agreement just brings us back to old questions. It is not enough to say that putting our beliefs in wide coherence will distinguish the more from the less reasonable. It will do that only if we can identify beliefs of high reliability. As we cannot do that without broaching some key metaethical questions, the independence of normative ethics is seriously compromised.

But can we, given the present state of philosophy, make progress in metaethics? Well, we now know so little about the nature and structure of our substantive ethical beliefs that we do not know whether the best moral view will, in the end, recommend itself to us because it meets epistemological standards or because it meets practical ones, such as its meshing effectively with the human will or its providing a much needed social consensus for us here and now. We may find that moral standards are what we agree between us to adopt as such, not what we discover independently to be such. Therefore, we cannot get far with meta-ethical questions about truth, objectivity, and realism until we have got clearer about the status that moral standards have in what turns out to be the best normative view. This argument of Rawls sees to me to have some force. But there is a second argument. For the reasons I have just given, we cannot get far with finding the best normative view until we have got clearer about what beliefs are highly reliable; and for that we need answers from metaethics. The combined effect of these two arguments is that sometimes the priority runs one way and sometimes the other. That is why I end the chapter by saying that normative ethics and metaethics have to advance together. The first is not independent of the second, or, as Rawls allows that the independence he has in mind is not especially strict (Rawls 1974–5: 5, 6, 21), there is nothing like the high degree of independence that he suggests.

34. I discuss the relation between normative ethics and metaethics in Griffin forthcoming *b*.

CHAPTER II

1. I shall come back to just how unsharp the cut is in Ch. V.
2. I have discussed prudential deliberation more fully in Griffin 1986: pt. i, and the ideas there were further worked in Griffin 1991*a* and Griffin 1992*b*. I shall therefore be fairly brief, and shall refer to those earlier discussions; in any case, parts of the last two I incorporate here.
3. The following two passages represent what I take to be common (typical?) views in economics. 'Our basic theory assumes first that, for all the alternative consumption bundles he could conceivably face, the individual has a preference ordering. This reflects his tastes. . . . from the opportunities available to him he does the best he can, best being defined according to his tastes' (Layard and Walters 1978: 124). 'The utility theory of choice states that the choice in any given situation depends on the interaction of the externally given obstacles [i.e. income and prices] with the *tastes* of the individual . . . The Utility theory asserts, more precisely, that the tastes can be represented by an ordering according to preference of all conceivable alternatives' (Arrow 1984: sect. entitled 'Choice Under Static Conditions'; his emphasis).

   Briefly, the situation in philosophy seems to be this. Hume explains all value—aesthetic, moral, prudential—on the taste model (see *A Treatise of Human Nature*, bk. III, pt. i). He sees reason as inert, able merely to inform us of how things stand; motivation and action come only from our conative response to those things.

   Kant follows Hume on prudence, but emphatically refuses to do so on morality. Many—I am one of them—think that there are good reasons to reject the taste model for moral values. Kant's reasons are these. We all want to be happy. But what would make us happy depends upon our particular desires, interests, inclinations, and dispositions. But they are the result of such contingencies as our biological make-up, the era into which we happen to have been born, the influence of our parents, and so on. They all operate on the phenomenal level; they grow, and get shaped entirely within the causal nexus. And we, so long as we are seen just on the level of desires, aims, and inclinations, are purely phenomenal selves, determined by things external to us—in Kant's term, heteronomous. What happens to us on that level is brute fact. It therefore offers no place for anything with the standing of a moral agent. We rise to the level of moral agency only when we manage to be autonomous, only when our actions are governed not by contingencies, but by self-given law. To be autonomous, Kant says, is 'to be independent of determination by causes in the sensible world' (Kant 1961: 120).

What I want to single out in this lightning exegesis is that Kant is quite clearly employing the taste model for many prudential values, but uses something like the perception model for moral standards. (I am stretching the perception model in including Kant. 'Perception' suggests detection or recognition of the presence of (moral) properties, and Kant is not a moral realist.) Kant stresses how varied our conceptions of happiness are—indeed, so varied that it is hard to see how to introduce some principled harmony between them and to see how to avoid another person's compelling me to be happy on his conception of welfare (Kant 1970: 73–4).

Confining the taste model to prudential values is widespread in contemporary philosophy. Rawls is strikingly like Kant in this respect. (For a fuller exploration of the parallels between Kant and Rawls, see Sandel 1982: esp. introduction, but also *passim*. Rawls himself spells out the parallels in Rawls 1972: sect. 40; he also offers corrections to Sandel's interpretation in Rawls 1985: n. 21.) Rawls treats our goals and aims as a matter of our psychology—in the end, the desires we come to have. When he talks about how a rational person chooses ends, this is the language he uses: a person's 'rational life plan' is the one that, if he were to reflect properly, he would be satisfied 'would best realize his more fundamental desires' (Rawls 1972: 417). Rawls's concern, it is true, is with a person's rational, not actual, desires, and there are important questions, to which I shall soon return, about how strong a requirement 'rational' has to be, and about when it becomes too strong to be kept within the confines of the taste model. But Rawls seems not to leave those confines; he speaks of 'deliberative rationality' in terms of a person's learning 'the general features of his wants and ends both present and future' and 'what he really wants', and of forms of 'criticizing our ends which may often help us to estimate the relative intensity of our desires' (ibid. 418–19; this, at any rate, seems to me to be the tenor of sect. 40 in particular and of the book in general). In sum, our prudential values express our contingent appetitive nature; our moral standards, on the other hand, express our nature as autonomous persons.

So Rawls's views seem to me to be typical of current thought: reject the taste model for moral values, but retain it for prudential values. The Humean tradition is still vigorous. But I doubt that the taste model explains prudential values either.

4. 'Thus the distinct boundaries and offices of *reason* and *taste* are easily ascertained. . . . The one discovers objects as they really stand in nature, without addition or diminution: the other has a productive faculty, and gilding or staining all natural objects with the colours, borrowed from internal sentiment, raises in a manner a new creation. Reason being cool and disengaged, is no motive to action . . . ; Taste, as it gives pleasure or pain, . . . becomes a motive to action' (App. I, *Enquiries*). There are modern employments of Hume's idea of values as human projections upon a value-neutral world: see Blackburn 1984: ch. 6 and (an especially elaborate development) Grice 1991: esp. Carus Lecture 3.

5. This is Richard Brandt's proposal in his 1979: 10.

6. This is Rawls's example in his 1972: 432-3.

7. Here I follow Simon Blackburn's discussion of Hume's essay: see Blackburn 1984: 199-202. The definition of 'a best possible set', which follows shortly in the text, is his; see p. 198.

8. Nor, I think, what Simon Blackburn's would be either. He adopts and embellishes Hume's account in his 1984: ch. 6, esp. sect. 3. See also Blackburn 1981: 186: 'Morally I think that we profit from the sentimentalist position by realising that a training of the feelings rather than a cultivation of a mysterious ability to spot the immutable fittingness of things is the foundation of knowing how to live.' This seems to me the unreal contrast between understanding and desire once again. Quite aside from his unsympathetic description of the realist position, Blackburn says nothing in this paper about how one 'trains' one's feelings. To explain this is to explain what prudential, moral, and aesthetic deliberation is like. Another explanation has the potential—realized, I think—to undercut the sentimentalist tradition.

9. Bernard Williams, in his paper 'Internal and External Reasons', also claims that there is no further scope, so the criticisms below apply to him as well. See Williams 1981: esp. 101-6. For a more adequate discussion of Williams's position, see Griffin 1986: 134-9.

10. John McDowell develops this line of thought in e.g. McDowell 1981; see also Simon Blackburn's (1981) reply in the same volume.

11. Simon Blackburn thinks that it is not; see Blackburn 1981. (I borrow the example of 'funny' from this article.) See also John McDowell's article in the same place, to which Blackburn was replying. Allan Gibbard supports Blackburn in Gibbard 1990: 112-17.

12. Similar points have been made throughout the history of philosophy. '[E]very action and decision seems to aim at some good; hence the good has been well described as that at which everything aims' (Aristotle, *Nicomachean Ethics*, 1094a); 'all that is required for our concept of "wanting" is that a man should see what he wants under the aspect of some good' (Anscombe 1957: 74).

13. This constraint applies to more than just the desires that appear in paradigmatic intentional actions; it applies indeed to most desires. But I doubt that it applies to all desires (e.g. to a post-hypnotic desire to do something pointless, like scratch one's un-itching head). For the view that it does, see e.g. Gauthier 1963: ch. 3, sect. 2; Stampe 1987; Sprigge 1988: ch. 6.

14. This is Thomas Nagel's position (and terminology). He once argued for my conclusion (in Nagel 1970: chs. 11–12), but later changed to this view (see Nagel 1986: ch. 8, sect. 5, and ch. 9, sects. 1–3; and Nagel 1991: ch. 2). I am concerned here only with prudential values. For a broader discussion of Nagel's position, see Korsgaard 1993.

15. See Nagel 1986. Some things 'acquire value only because of the interest we develop in them' (p. 168). 'Their value is not impersonally detachable, because it is too bound up with the idiosyncratic aims and attitudes of the subject, and can't be subsumed under a more universal value of comparable importance, like that of pleasure and pain' (ibid.). Our personal reasons for action stem from the 'system of preference of the agent' (p. 170).

16. This is Nagel's question too (see Nagel 1991: 16).

17. See esp. Chs. VI, VII, and VIII. Nagel sees another important role for personal values. In general, impersonal values or disvalues (e.g. pain) set up claims on others to aid, whereas personal values or disvalues, being more subject to a person's choice, do not create claims so readily (Nagel 1986: 166–7). This, then, would help keep the interests of others from building up to claims that swamped one's own personal concerns. But personal values are instances of impersonal ones; if playing the piano well is the way in which I can accomplish something with my life, then it is no more an option that I can or cannot choose than making something out of my life is. And once the distinction between the two kinds of values weakens in this way, so too do the implications about aid. I say more about this in Griffin 1986: Ch. III. Swamping is, of course, a problem. So we must find some other solution.

18. This list of values does not assign enjoyment, or any other single item, special, fundamental standing, the value to which all other values can be reduced. I doubt that any substantive value has this role. But that does not mean that commensuration or maximization of values is impossible. It is just a mistake to think that commensurability of prudential values needs a supreme substantive prudential value. All that it needs is that 'prudential value' itself be a quantitative notion—that is, that it be able to figure in judgements as to 'more', 'less', or 'same' value, which it can. I discuss the (in)commensurability of values more fully in Griffin 1986: Ch. V; Griffin 1991b; and Griffin forthcoming a.

19. I speak as if there were *one* list—whatever, in the end, might be on it. I shall say more about what goes into judgements about membership of the list in Chs. III and IV. But many people would protest already at this point that we must accept not just pluralism of prudential values, but also pluralism of valuable forms of life (which, however, is compatible with a single list of prudential values) and pluralism of lists of values (which, of course, is not). As for the last form of pluralism, many would say that the values on various lists are themselves incommensurable. My own list is very much out of a particular tradition: modern, Western, and atheist. But take someone with a radically different list: instead of enjoyment, the mortification of the flesh; instead of deep personal relations, cloistered solitude; instead of autonomy, submission to the will of God. But of course one's list will change with one's metaphysical views. If I believed in a certain kind of God, I too might have a different list. But this makes lists relative not to culture, but (unsurprisingly) to one's judgements about the world one thinks one is living in. Or take a Homeric hero's list: strength, physical courage, political persuasiveness, excellence of girth and body (see Snare 1992: 122). But some lists are not so much lists of ends of life (what makes an individual life worthwhile) as of ideals of life (qualities that one looks for in individuals). If I lived in a warrior society, I too might regard these as desirable features. The qualities that one values because they are needed in a particular social setting are bound to change as social conditions change. But this does not show that these lists contain incommensurably different values. Imagine what a Buddhist aiming at the extinction of desire would think of my highly ambitious end 'accomplishment'. The Buddha was right that we open ourselves to suffering by being attached to things, many of which are unnecessary. But a few attachments might be worth the pain; we have to decide. A pain-free life excludes deep personal relations and most accomplishments, but the incompatibility of values is not their incommensurability. This whole subject needs a book of its own. I discuss it further in Griffin 1986, Griffin 1991*b*, and Griffin forthcoming *a*.

20. See e.g. Gordon 1987: chs. 4, 5; Gibbard 1990: ch. 7.

21. My objections to these dualisms echo those of early critics of the Enlightenment. The Enlightenment conception of the human agent centres on a series of sharp distinctions: fact/value, reason/sentiment, understanding/reaction, subjective/objective. They are common to e.g. both Hume and Kant. Critics of the Enlightenment, going back at least to Kant's immediate successors, attacked these sharp distinctions (see Taylor 1975: ch. 1, esp. pp. 13–29). But despite this, the Enlightenment view generally prevailed, a success that had much to

do with its critics' excesses. This history leaves us now with the job of finding a different vocabulary with which to advance the subject. I return to these matters in my final chapter.

CHAPTER III

1. This is Moore's first suggestion in Moore 1903: 40; he there explains the 'natural' as 'that which is the subject-matter of the natural sciences and also psychology'.
2. Ibid. 41.
3. See Moore 1942: 588. Thomas Baldwin thinks that this interpretation of the distinction is already present, in a confused way, in the *Principia Ethica* discussion; see Baldwin 1985: 30.
4. For it to be reductivist, it must also claim that the terms in the *definiens* are more basic than those in the *definiendum*; equivalence (in sense) is two-way reduction, and we want one-way.
5. On that ground for doubt, see e.g. Railton 1989: 157–9.
6. Ziff 1960: ch. 6; Katz 1964.
7. Ziff 1960: ch. 6, esp. p. 218.
8. R. B. Brandt makes this reduction, effected by a 'reforming definition' of prudential value, in these psychological terms. See Brandt 1979: Ch. I, sect. 2. See also my earlier discussion of Brandt in Ch. I, n. 7. Although Brandt's naturalism starts with a reforming definition, it still seems to be 'substantive' rather than 'conceptual'. He does not offer an analysis of our current value-concepts; he offers a view about what empirical matters values comes down to.
9. This is Peter Railton's aim in Railton 1986, in which he adopts an informed-desire account, but regards the result as a kind of naturalism. See esp. sect. 3.
10. Railton would, I think, regard my account of the sensitivity as being too rich; he keeps his account spare enough to pass as a form of naturalism. But that it is too spare shows itself, it seems to me, in various ways. He explains prudential value as, roughly, what a person would want to want when fully informed (see sect. 3, esp. pp. 174–8). But this does not solve the problem of excessive breadth: we want things when fully informed (e.g. the success of the stranger we meet on the train, or the well-being of our twenty-second-century successors) that, if realized, do not enhance our personal lives at all. Furthermore, Railton's account, being restricted to a certain sort of causal interaction (viz. such-and-such features of objects produce, in a state of full knowledge etc., a reaction of desire), leaves out the reason-giving side of what is going on: that certain features are life-enhancing, that

they constitute reasons for action rooted in a person's good. Certain features of objects are desirability features, features generally recognizable as human aims—such as enjoyment, accomplishment, and so on. Railton's relational account concentrates exclusively on the fact that, in certain circumstances (e.g. full knowledge), one's desires become such-and-such. Well, what is so special about *that* pattern of desires? Why should those desires have any authority over action? The explanation has to be in terms of reasons for action of a special sort: namely, that fulfilment of these desires makes one's life better. The facts that Railton stresses about causal interaction resulting in desire are indeed objective in the sense that Railton wants, but they do not go far enough to explain prudential value. We need mention of desirability features and an explanation of their status. And once they enter the picture, we have a solution to the first difficulty: the success of the stranger on the train and people's flourishing in the twenty-second century, though both qualifying as what we should want to want, are not subsumable under one or other of the right sort of value-headings. But once this complication enters the picture, the issue of realism about values becomes more difficult, I think, than Railton makes it.

11. Freud 1957: 138. See the interesting discussion of Freudian explanations of value and obligation in Wollheim 1984: esp. 204–5, 215–16; much of its interest is how extraordinarily thin this psychological explanation is, even in Wollheim's sensitive hands.

12. e.g. Harman 1977: ch. 1 and Harman 1985. Mackie approaches this position; see his 1977: ch. 5.

13. For an early version of the proposal, see Hare 1952: 80 ff., 131. See also Ross 1930: 116–23. For a more recent statement of the proposal, see Hare 1984b.

14. 'Dependence': see e.g. Davidson 1980: 214: 'mental characteristics are in some sense dependent, or supervenient, on physical characteristics.' 'Underlying': see Blackburn 1984: 182: 'The idea is that some properties, the A-properties, are consequential upon some other base properties, the underlying B-properties.' 'Consequential': see the previous quotation from Blackburn, also Hare 1963: 19: 'moral properties do not vary quite independently of non-moral properties, but are in some sense consequential or supervenient on them.' See also Hare 1952: 80.

15. See e.g. Goldman 1988: 134, where supervenience is defined as 'the requirement that we not make different moral judgements when we cannot find differences in non-moral judgements (and furthermore, that we take the latter differences to be generally morally relevant)'.

16. However, 'true in virtue of' does not have to take a truth-bearer as its second term: e.g. an analytic proposition is true in virtue of the

meaning of its terms. This dependence of truth upon meaning is different from the sort of dependence, with potential ontological implications, that we usually have in mind with values and natural facts, mental states and brain states, etc. So 'true in virtue of' can be used of different kinds of relation. See Charles and Lennon 1992: 16–18.

17. Grice 1991: esp. Carus Lecture 3. Grice sees empirical science as 'hypothesizing', metaphysics as 'hypostasizing'. I gather that he would be prepared to distinguish science from metaphysics by appeal to their different procedures, those of the latter being 'Humean Projection', 'Category Shift' and 'Metaphysical Transubstantiation' (pp. 107–15), though he also has hopes for a more systematic approach to the distinction (p. 71).

CHAPTER IV

1. 'The Last Testament of Bertrand Russell', *Independent*, London, 24 Nov. 1993, p. 21.
2. Grice 1991: 81–8, 111–15.
3. The analogy between sensitivity to values and perception is proposed and explored by John McDowell in a justly well-known paper (1985). McDowell's analogy with, in particular, the perception of secondary qualities has been criticized—with force, I think—in e.g. Dancy 1993: 156–63 and Wright 1988. In any case, the analogy with secondary qualities is not needed to explore the issues that McDowell used it to explore: viz. what is subjective in value judgement, and what objective, and how the subjectivity can be compatible with the objectivity.
4. 'Soothing' is not what John Locke would call a primary quality of the ointment or the tone of voice that is soothing; the ointment and the tone of voice have that effect, but there is nothing *in* either that resembles, in the rather obscure sense of that term that Locke intends, the physical or psychological response it produces in us. It is not even what Locke would call a secondary quality; it is, rather, what he fleetingly refers to as a tertiary property—a mere power that something has to produce an effect in us, such as a fire's causing us pain if we get too close, which we do not regard as among the standard properties of the thing. See Locke, *Essay Concerning Human Understanding*, bk. II, ch. 8, esp. sects. 6–10.
5. For a well-thought-out example of the latter position, see Blackburn 1984: ch. 6, sect. 3, 'Constructing Truth'.
6. This way of articulating the realist intuition is in some ways unsatisfactory. Talk of the existence of 'things' or 'entities' suits realism about physical objects better than other forms of realism. And if we

let ourselves be too influenced by the model of physical reality, then we shall expect moral realism to require either Platonism or a belief in a 'value realm' perceived by a quasi-perceptive faculty of 'intuition'. But we can guard against this distortion by allowing properties as well as entities to be real. To say that something is prudentially valuable is to say that it is, or meets, a human interest. And being, or meeting, an interest seems more in the category of a property than of an individual bearer of properties. Another unsatisfactory feature of this articulation of the realist intuition is its making realism a matter of independence of the mental. Yet reality includes, besides rocks and chairs, people. People have minds. How, then, can real things be defined as independent of the mental? The answer, I think, is that the independence in question is a thing's independence of, not any awareness or belief, but specifically awareness or belief about *it*. A thought might be merely a brain state accompanied by a certain phenomenological feel—i.e. an awareness of the thought. But then again, a thought might be something independent of both the brain state and the phenomenological feel. This articulation of realism, I think, rules out neither.

7. For a critical discussion of the 'best explanation' test, see Wright 1992: ch. 5.

8. It looks that way to Thomas Nagel (1986: 144).

9. This, I think, arouses the doubt as to whether I, in particular, can adopt the causal test. Can I consistently adopt the test, yet deny that values supervene on the natural—on the Humean conception of the 'natural'? If values interact with other things causally, and if causal interaction is a matter of regularities of operation of the Humean natural world, then there must, it would seem, be the sort of connection between Humean natural facts and values that supervenience asserts. But this point just assumes that values, unreduced, cannot enter causal relations.

10. David Wiggins, e.g., spurns my sort of test of best causal explanation, on which one looks for causation between states of affairs and our concepts or beliefs. He prefers a test of 'vindicatory explanation': we have a vindicatory explanation of why A believes that *p* if and only if the modes of assessment appropriate to the particular domain of discourse in which *p* is expressed leave us nothing else to think but that *p*, and A's belief that *p* is formed in accordance with those modes of assessment. See Wiggins 1987: esp. essays II–V, and Wiggins 1990–1. Many beliefs in mathematics, such as that $7 + 5 = 12$, can pass this test. But the doubt is whether the test is strong enough to ensure the sort of independence of belief that realism intuitively requires. It may deliver a kind of objectivity—but does it deliver anything worth

calling realism? On that question see Wright 1992: ch. 5, sect. 3. (Not, perhaps, that Wiggins would mind if it did not; his interest is less in 'realism' than in, as he puts it, restoring and making good 'the cognitive aspiration of moral judgement': see Wiggins 1990–1: 64; but see also his claims for the reality of moral properties, pp. 84–5.)

11. David Wiggins makes this point in 'Truth, and Truth as Predicated of Moral Judgements', in Wiggins 1987.

12. This is a contentious point; see Griffin 1986: Ch. I, sect. 5, and Ch. II, sect. 1.

CHAPTER V

1. I have discussed this more fully in Ch. II, sect. 1.

2. Wittgenstein is the one who made this clear; see his 1953: sects. 243–308.

3. I discussed whether motivation is internal to the recognition of an interest earlier, in Ch. II, sect. 6. Not surprisingly, it is hard to articulate at all fully how our phenomenological feels and our responses to them work together in our concept of 'pain'. The linguistic phenomena to be explained are complex. Some lobotomized subjects have said that they feel pain without wanting to avoid or alleviate it. Are such responses then necessary to something's being a 'pain'? Is 'pain' just a phenomenological feel? Is 'suffering', not 'pain', what I should be interested in? As to the last, it would not matter to me if it were. But I think that the account of 'pain' I have given in the text can stand. Apart from the question of how we should interpret the reports of some lobotomized patients, it remains the case that we could not explain our use of 'pain' without appeal to both phenomenological feels and characteristic responses. That must be the normal case, upon which abnormal cases are parasitic. The responses on their own are not enough: we wish to avoid or alleviate much more than pains. The phenomenological feels are not enough: there is a large variety of them, and we need a way to bring them together under one concept. There are good discussions of the issues in Hare 1981: ch. 5, sect. 2; and Sumner 1992.

4. This is also the gist of Thomas Nagel's case (1986: 159–62), about which he justly remarks: 'this conclusion seems to me self-evident, and in trying to explain why it is true . . . I may not have gone far beyond this' (p. 162). Derek Parfit's much fuller discussion of self-interest (Parfit 1984: sects. 1–9, 32–40, 45–74) heads in the same general direction as mine, though he leaves the conclusion more open than I do.

5. That apparent impregnability is the source of Sidgwick's pessimism about the whole enterprise of practical rationality: we clearly have both self-interested and other-interested reasons, but seem to have no way to bring them together. See Sidgwick 1907: Concluding Chapter. Mackie (1976) defends Sidgwick's conclusion against, e.g. Moore (1903: sects. 59–61).

6. e.g. Sidgwick 1903: 111–12, 127–9, 396–8, who conceives of it as 'desirable consciousness'.

7. If we take educated egoism as setting the proper standard for an egoist, as of course we must, then it follows that, as we are genetically programmed to be primitively egoistic, we are genetically programmed to be to some degree *imprudent.*

8. This point is strikingly illustrated by Oliner and Oliner 1988, who recount cases in which extraordinary concern for others was combined with, and to some extent carried by, a robust respect for self.

9. On the primacy of ethics, see Williams 1985: chs. 1 and 10; Raz 1986: ch. 12, sect. 6; Hurley 1989: ch. 8, sect. 4.

10. For an interesting answer with a somewhat different focus from mine, see Gibbard 1990.

11. Mackie 1977: 41.

12. See Ch. II, sect. 1.

CHAPTER VI

1. Bernard Williams, 'Persons, Character and Morality', and 'Utilitarianism and Self-Indulgence', in Williams 1981; also 'A Critique of Utilitarianism', in Smart and Williams 1973: sects. 3, 5. There is much that Williams says about integrity with which I disagree, but this, his central point, seems to me right and important. Sprigge develops the same theme illuminatingly in 1988: 181 ff. See Updike 1990: 201.

2. For the distinction between 'crude' and 'educated' self-interest, see Ch. V, sect. 3.

3. See Sprigge 1988: 181–2.

4. This is Shelly Kagan's answer in 1989: ch. 8. I argue against this answer in much the same terms as here in my review of Kagan's book, Griffin 1990.

5. For her chief statement, see Murdoch 1970. See also a profile of her in the *Independent,* London, 29 Apr. 1989.

6. Profile, *Independent,* 29 Apr. 1989.

7. Murdoch 1970: esp. 92–4. Reinhold Niebuhr's position, in his paper 'The Relevance of an Impossible Ethical Ideal' (in Niebuhr 1956), seems to me the plausible one for a religious believer. He says that

the ethic of love requires more than the normal human frame can deliver. He also thinks—as against Iris Murdoch—that nothing is going to happen in human life to change that. '[T]he moral experience at any level of life points toward an unrealizable breadth of obligation of life to life' (p. 106). However, at the same time as allowing this, he wants still to claim 'the relevance of the love commandment'. How then does he reconcile its relevance with its impossibility? 'In Christian theology, at its best, the revelation of Christ, the God-man, is a revelation of the paradoxical relation of the eternal to history, which it is the genius of mythical-prophetic religion to emphasize. Christ is thus the revelation of the very impossible possibility which the Sermon on the Mount elaborates in ethical terms' (p. 111). But this resolution is of no help to the non-believer.

8. In contrast to the expectations of some religious believers. The Archbishop of Canterbury, Dr George Carey, has said that although atheists could live sober, honest, and fruitful lives, they were unlikely to go beyond those bounds into the sort of truly selfless behaviour exemplified by Mother Teresa; if they did so, they were acting as if they were believers, not as true atheists. Lecture reported in the *Independent*, 5 June 1992.

9. The words are from a speech made by Chai Ling, which became the manifesto of the hunger-strikers: '[E]ven though death, to us, is too heavy a burden to bear, we have decided to take our leave. We have no choice but to take our leave. History demands this from us . . . We use courage that enables us to face death, to fight for the life that's worth living. . . . We do not want to die. . . . Because the best times of our lives are yet before us, we really do not want to die. . . . However, if one person's death, or a few people's deaths, can enable more people to lead better lives, and can help our nation to become more prosperous, we then have not the right to continue living stealthily. . . . Farewell, beloved, take care! I cannot bear to take leave of you, yet there is no choice but to take leave' (quoted in Lu 1990: 131–2).

10. Li Lu, one of the student leaders in Tiananmen Square, remarks: '[T]he grim society of China did not give me the chance to understand and pursue life. I thought of Chai Ling's words: "We use courage that defies death to fight for the life that's worth living." I remembered the words of the four intellectuals: "We do not seek death; we seek genuine life"' (Lu 1990: 211).

11. This explanation of 'can't' may look culture-bound. It may still seem to rest on modern Western conceptions of 'suitable settled dispositions', 'sustainable social order', and even 'human norms'. Take a culture radically different from ours precisely in ways relevant to

self-sacrifice—say a Buddhist society aiming at the extinction of self-centred desires (the third of the Four Noble Truths). But Buddhism also recognizes the limits on how far this extinction can go, and accordingly accepts a middle way between a life of worldly ambition and a fully ascetic life. See the discussion in Flanagan 1991: 76–7.

12. What I suggest here might be called a 'psychological' solution to the problem that ethics is unrealistically demanding: 'ought' implies 'can', and we can do only so much. Some think that psychological solutions are unnecessary, because morality itself provides the solution: e.g. morality stands for justice, and so morality itself requires us to do only our fair share. It would ask us to give only that amount of money to save the starving that, if everyone were to do the same (whether or not they actually will), would be enough. But moral requirements do not seem to be like that. If you and I were crossing a bridge over a pond and to the left one child was drowning and to the right another one was, and if I were to panic and run off, then you could not say, having waded in and saved one, that you could go on your way because you have done your fair share.

13. Philosophers differ sharply about it, because they have very different hunches about human nature. John Mackie asks: '[I]s it intended that each agent should take the happiness of all as his goal? This, surely, is too much to expect.' And he calls act utilitarianism 'the ethics of fantasy' (Mackie 1977: 129). To which Derek Parfit replies: 'We may *hope* that the best theory is not unrealistically demanding. But on these views [i.e. views about the nature of morality other than Mackie's own belief that we invent right and wrong], this can only be a hope. We cannot assume that this must be true' (Parfit 1984: 29). I once wrote that Mackie's gibe about 'the ethics of fantasy' largely misunderstood utilitarianism (Griffin 1986: 185), but since then my hunch about human nature has changed.

Of course, there is also, on the other side, a great danger of underestimating human plasticity. Much depends upon social conditioning, and no doubt society should aim at producing citizens of ampler sympathies than most people now have. Much depends too upon one's conception of one's own responsibility for what happens to strangers. Jonathan Glover writes: 'It is possible to speculate that these limitations of emotional involvement [roughly our present ones] were relatively unimportant in the environment of primitive man. Concern restricted to a few people, and to what happens nearby in space and time, is adequate for people whose actions have effects limited in the same way. But now we can kill or save lives at a distance and greatly influence the lives of future generations' (Glover 1977: 294; but see more generally ch. 20, sects. 4 and 5).

14. I give my own views about it more fully in Griffin 1986: Ch. X.

15. But we should not carry this line of thought back so far that it is seen as the reason for moving from the state of nature to that of society. If there were no norms, standards, conventions, or institutions, human life would not be worse than it otherwise might be: it would simply not be recognizable as human life. The picture of a normless state of nature is (close to?) incoherent. If there were no conventions and associated norms, there would be no language, which is essentially normative. If there were no language, there would be no articulable reasons. We start already inside society; we do not find reasons to move to it, even if such a move were regarded as purely hypothetical. Political philosophy's besetting sin is over-intellectualizing, over-rationalizing, society and its norms. Society and many of its key norms are a natural growth, a setting within which, and only within which, we can debate the pros and cons of features of our social life.

16. Despite my mention of reform, this view may sound unattractively conservative. But it need not be. It is consistent with thinking that many contemporary systems of property, e.g., need major changes. But when property laws are changed to allow a decent minimum social provision, when privileged positions are open to all, and when certain other not unfamiliar changes are made, we reach the sort of institution of property that I have in mind. See the discussion in Ch. VII, sect. 9.

CHAPTER VII

1. Some, or all, of these cases have been discussed, e.g., by Philippa Foot, 'The Problem of Abortion and the Doctrine of the Double Effect', in Foot 1978; by Jonathan Bennett (1981: esp. 75–7); Judith Jarvis Thomson (1975–6; 1990: esp. chs. 5–7); Shelly Kagan (1989: esp. chs. 3 and 4). The cabin-boy case is based on an actual nineteenth-century incident, the aftermath of the sinking of the *Mignonette* (see Simpson 1984).

2. Today we use this example a good deal more uneasily than did its originators. What was meant as a fantastic case is now probably reality. A recent judicial investigation in Argentina studied evidence that doctors at a mental hospital outside Buenos Aires had murdered patients in order to sell their blood and organs. From 1976 to 1991 nearly 1,400 patients were classed by the hospital as having 'disappeared', presumably escaped, but none has ever reappeared. The body of one patient, Marcello Ortiz, a totally paralyzed 16-year-old said by the hospital to have escaped, was found in a well near the

hospital with his eyes missing (report in *The Guardian*, 14 Apr. 1992). The BBC reports that in China organs are taken from executed prisoners, supposedly with their consent, for sale for transplant, raising the fear that benefit for the ailing rich and powerful will interfere with clemency for the offenders. It reports too on a brisk trade in organs, especially with Arab countries, in India, where the poor sell their kidneys to escape from debt (the going price is about three times their annual income) (*Assignment*: The Great Organ Bazaar, BBC2, 23 June 1992). When important moral inhibitions are in good repair, we can talk about these cases without misgiving. But now we wonder whether, or how, philosophy may have contributed to their present disrepair. See also n. 4 below.

3. I borrow the distinction between 'promoting' and 'respecting' values from Philip Pettit (1991), though he uses the terms 'promoting' and 'honouring'. See also n. 7 below.

4. And would be morally right to do it? If, all things considered, something is the reasonable thing to do, is it then morally permitted? Or might one, all things considered, have reason to do something immoral? I say the first, as I think most philosophers do. If that all-things-considered judgement were not brought into the moral sphere, we should just need a larger sphere of the permitted. But the way we choose to talk about this bears on the question of keeping important moral inhibitions in good repair. Our moral inhibitions might get in bad repair by our making thinkable (a matter of argument, calculation, weighing) what should not be. Might it be better to see the problem facing the shipwrecked sailors in the cabin-boy case *not* as a moral one, but as a wrenching conflict between the demands of morality and the demands of survival? To see the prohibition on killing the cabin-boy as an immensely high barrier, without any moral ladders available to help, would have the effect of driving the sailors to the extremes of practical ingenuity, of not giving in until everything else was exhausted. Yes, the answer will be, but suppose everything else has been exhausted. It is, of course, a theoretical possibility; but one effect of stressing this theoretical possibility might be to make us move more briskly to this extreme point in practice. Were the doctors in Argentina already doing that (see n. 2)? I am much indebted to Susan Khin Zaw for correspondence on this point. I shall come back to the crucial matter of keeping inhibitions in repair later in the chapter.

5. There is the large question of rational strategies in the face of great ignorance. When we answer that question, might we not find indirect utilitarianism reappearing? Is my point about, say, a fairly satisfactory institution of property simply that, given how little we know about

the costs and benefits at stake in highly complex social institutions, the best policy is 'Better the devil you know'. That looks like indirect utilitarianism, because it looks like the plausible thought that our particular institution of property has at least stood the test of time. If that is simply the thought that we have to abandon maximization in these cases, then it is well short of indirect utilitarianism. But if it is the thought that our abandoning maximization is ultimately the maximizing thing to do, then I doubt that we can tell.

6. Here is one attempt at giving it support. What interests there are is an objective matter. All that one needs in order to move from these objective goods to moral right is a function attaching weights to the good of different individuals. One function, maximization, is salient; it rests on the truth of the principle: If x (say, pleasure or happiness) is good, more is better. This yields a criterion of moral right and wrong, independent of our knowledge of it.

But maximization, as I have argued elsewhere (Griffin 1986: Ch. IX), is not in this way salient. There are many functions all capable of carrying us from objective goods to moral right (maximization, equalization, Rawls's difference principle, etc.) and all with some intuitive appeal. Maximization can look salient because it can be confused with the principle above: If x is good, more is better. On that truistic interpretation, though, maximization is merely a standard for ranking outcomes: it has not yet got enough content to be a moral standard for action. For it to be that, one has to take a further, fateful decision as to when benefiting one person justifies harming another—when, say, I have a reason to help you at the cost of helping my children. One needs more than that principle to get us to a decision on this matter. And that one needs more opens up a crucial space in which human capacities might play a role.

7. I want to add something, even if equally speedily, about consequentialism. Consequentialism differs from utilitarianism, one of its species, mainly in the greater breadth of its value theory. Utilitarians assess outcomes by looking at individual well-being. Consequentialists look either at well-being or at moral goods, such as equality, respect for rights, fidelity to one's word, and so on, or indeed, and commonly, at both.

Even on this much broadened value theory, there remains an important difference between consequentialists and non-consequentialists. Consequentialists, as I put it earlier, hold that values are to be promoted (e.g. maximized), whereas non-consequentialists hold that some values are to be respected. For instance, an innocent person's right not to be killed is one of the values that could fall under the broadened consequentialist conception. Consequentialists respond to this value by bringing about its respect generally—say, by minimizing violations of the right in society at large—that is, by promoting it. Non-consequentialists respond by respecting it themselves in their own behaviour. (It is not easy, however, to find a comprehensive, entirely trouble-free formulation of the distinction between consequentialism and non-consequentialism. For troubles with the formulation in terms of promoting and respecting (or promoting and honouring, as Philip Pettit puts it—see n. 3), see McNaughton and Rawlings 1991–2. There are troubles too, I think, with formulating the distinction in terms of agent-neutral and agent-relative reasons or obligations. In any case, I shall try to formulate the two forms of consequentialism that I want shortly to discuss in specific enough terms to make the difference between each of them and its corresponding form of non-consequentialism tolerably clear.)

Despite their differences, my earlier doubts about utilitarianism carry over to consequentialism. Let me look first at a broad form of consequentialism, and next at a narrower—and, to my mind, much more plausible—form.

Some consequentialists broaden the conception of good to include *acts* of fairness, of promise-keeping, of respect for rights, and so on. A consequentialist of this type, that is, adopts the goal of promoting these acts generally, whose ever they are. This seems to me a good place to start, because it shows, I think, how easily nowadays we write into ethics goals that connect so tenuously to our capacities.

Admittedly, one person might just be able to violate someone's right to life in a way that leads many others autonomously to respect the right when, otherwise, they would not have. It would, though, have to be a thoroughly exceptional situation. Suppose that a leading Mafia hit man with a change of heart realizes that if he were to make one last, spectacularly brutal hit, he could so disgust enough of his fellow hit men that he would reduce Mafia murders overall. He might be able to work a kind of conversion. But how often are such conversions within one's power? It would probably be a unique chance for the Mafia hit man, so it would be unreasonable of him to elevate his response to this one case to a policy for his whole moral life. I doubt that I have ever been in such a position, even in promoting more everyday matters such as acts of fairness or promise-keeping. Nor, I suspect, have most people. Normal agents are not. If I, situated as I am, were to break a promise or act unfairly with the aim of bringing about more cases of autonomous promise-keeping or fairness, then, unlike the Mafia hit man, I should merely be dropping my act into a causal stream in which so many other eddies and currents and undertows are at work that I could have, at best, only the faintest hope of producing the desired effect. Thus, though such conversions are not psychologically impossible, they are so rare, so unlikely ever to present themselves in the course of life, so much a fluke of fate, as, for all practical purposes, not to figure in the formation of our goals in life. 'Ought' implies 'can'. All moral theories work implicitly with a picture of what lies within human capacity. But acts such as maximizing the universal observance of promise-keeping or of fairness are simply not in our repertoire. Our moral life is not so much a matter of what we do as of what we choose to do. I do not have to be 100 per cent sure of bringing it off. I can, for instance, choose to go to London first thing tomorrow morning, although British Rail might let me down. But if the chances are only one in several million of my carrying something off, then I cannot be said to choose to do it. I can choose to have a flutter on the National Lottery, but not to win it. Winning may enter my hopes and plans, but not my intentions. The chances of my promise-breaking or acting unfairly making others (plural) autonomously keep their promises or act fairly approach National Lottery proportions. There is, therefore, something quite unreal in consequentialists' choosing as one of their goals in life, Promote promise-keeping impartially, Promote just acts impartially. It is not the sort of action-guiding goal that one would ever give to, or adopt as, an agent.

Still, breaking one's own promise or acting unfairly oneself is not the only means at one's disposal for influencing others. One can persuade or indoctrinate. But this addition to our causal resources may marginally expand, but does not radically alter, our prospects of success. Few of us are in a position to persuade or indoctrinate effectively. I was when my children were young, but a person's moral character is pretty much fixed in childhood, and little, certainly not sermons or lectures, is likely to change it afterward. The Mafia hit man's making a speech in favour of respect for life would have little chance of success. My making a similar speech would have even less. The strangeness of the goal remains.

What is strange is, precisely, these broad consequentialists' choosing as goals in life the population-wide promotion of autonomous acts of promise-keeping, acts of justice, respect for rights, and the like. It is not at all strange that opportunities for conversions are rare. After all, opportunities for saving babies who fall face down into puddles are rare too. Still, one can choose as a goal helping others in distress when the cost to oneself is small, and saving a baby in a puddle fits under this heading. Although that particular case is rare, cases of that kind certainly are not, and acts of compliance with the principle are within our powers. What makes a moral principle strange, however, is not the rarity of one particular instantiation of the kind of situation it regulates (there is nothing strange in that), but the unlikelihood of being able to comply with it at all. Why choose a standard for moral action so remotely connected with what one can do? Of course, 'strange' does not imply 'wrong'. But 'ought' does imply 'can'. Action-guiding principles must fit human capacities, or they become strange in a damaging way: namely, pointless.

Of course, broad consequentialists, like utilitarians, have resources for reply. They could, in parallel to a move that utilitarians make, say that their promotion of acts of fairness and of promise-keeping is meant not as a decision procedure, but as a criterion of right and wrong. But I doubt that this is any more successful with consequentialism than it was with utilitarianism. I spoke in the last chapter about strong demands (say, Jesus's saying: 'Be ye therefore perfect') that may go too far beyond our capacity even to be moral criteria. In certain respects, the promotion of promise-keeping or fairness is more remote from human capacities than is perfection. In seeking perfection, the problem is to make one's own recalcitrant will conform. In promoting promise-keeping or fairness, the problem is to make an altogether more independent world conform. If it is strained to say that one 'intends' to promote promise-keeping or acts of fairness, it is also strained to say that one will 'try' to promote them. Unless one can afford to buy a great number of tickets, one cannot 'try' to win the National Lottery either.

That is not the end of a broad consequentialist's replies, but let me, none the less, stop here. I have written more about it elsewhere (Griffin 1992a). There is a bad fit between the idea of promoting value generally and these moral values—such as acts of promise-keeping—that get added in the widening process that defines broad consequentialism. It involves a very odd conception of agency. It is hard enough to keep one's own moral inhibitions in good repair; it is hard enough to behave half-way decently oneself. To take as one's aim the promotion of good behaviour in humanity at large seems both to mistake the main ethical battleground and to make defeat there more likely. This broad sort of consequentialism seems to turn ethics into a project that ill-suits the agents who are meant to carry it out. Besides, quite apart from the capacity of agents, there is something quite odd about wishing to promote *acts* of fairness, of promise-keeping, and the rest. Would anyone care about the number of such acts in abstraction from their importance? For instance, is it better to have ten fair things done rather than five, if the ten concern minor matters and the five major ones? Do we not, if we are decent, want to promote our own and other persons' goals fairly, and perhaps also fairness itself, rather than *acts* of fairness?

The much more plausible forms of consequentialism are narrower ones—ones, in particular, that drop the emphasis on promoting acts. They might include among goods, besides prudential values, such moral states of affairs as fair procedures and equal distribution. What seems to me a particularly appealing form would include also *opportunities* to realize prudential values. For instance, an attractive solution to the free-rider problem can be found by adopting as one's aim equalizing people's chances at well-being (see e.g. Griffin 1986: Ch. X, sects. 3–5). Or, instead of making equality part of the maximand, one could make it an alternative to maximizing. One could confine what is to be promoted to well-being, as utilitarians do, but broaden the range of functions that can be used to move from good to right: they might include, besides maximizing well-being, equalizing it among people, or equalizing it except when inequalities work to the advantage of the worst off, or raising people to some minimum acceptable level of well-being above which obligations cease, and so on. These narrower forms of consequentialism make equality and fairness into entirely feasible goals. I can write a cheque to Oxfam. I can campaign with the rest of you against racial discrimination. There is nothing impossible about any of that.

But these narrower forms of consequentialism still raise doubts —the same sorts of doubts that utilitarianism does. Can we do the extraordinarily complex calculations of costs and benefits at their centre often enough, and to a sufficient degree of reliability, for the whole project to be feasible? There is an enormous number of possible forms of consequentialism, so it is even more pertinent to it than to utilitarianism that the strength of this worry depends upon the particular form in question. A possible form of consequentialism, though not a particularly compelling one, would concentrate exclusively on promoting equality, and with that goal the burden of calculation would be eased. One would need to identify only differences in welfare between people, and that would not require calculating even individual welfare levels. But the most plausible form of consequentialism, I should say, is one that aims at promoting a variety of goods, including not only equality, but also fairness and well-being (a good example is Scanlon 1978). Even the much more demanding calculations that this sort of consequentialism requires will sometimes be possible to a reliable degree of probability. But sometimes, also, they will not be. And we have to decide whether the failures in calculation occur often enough, and at central enough points in our moral life, for narrow consequentialism to lose any claim to be the overall form of moral rationality. The pressures on us to adopt an indirect form of utilitarianism would recur here too. So the central question in morality would be something along these lines: What set of rules and dispositions would, over society at large and in the long run, most promote well-being, fairness, and equality, and how are these competing goods to be weighed against one another? Like utilitarianism, consequentialist system is, to my mind, too ambitious. It cannot be the universal, overarching form of moral reasoning—not even the all-sanctioning background form of that reasoning.

There are, of course, still other forms of consequentialism. It may be that, in pushing the promotion of good into the background by making it the criterion of right and wrong, we have not pushed it quite far enough or back to the right place. The most interesting forms of consequentialism in future, I think, will be those that give it a different background place, without pushing it so far into the background that nothing worth calling 'consequentialism' remains. It is a difficult balance to strike. For possibilities, see Warnock 1971 and Mackie 1977, who regard the betterment of human life as the object of the whole apparatus of morality, rather than as the goal of moral action, though this may go too far to be any kind of 'consequentialism'. But see also the view that Allan Gibbard shows some sympathy with in the final chapter of Gibbard 1990.

8. Elizabeth Anscombe considers this identification a feature of 'the Hebrew–Christian ethic': 'it has been characteristic of that ethic to teach that there are certain things forbidden whatever *consequences* threaten, such as: choosing to kill the innocent for any purpose, however good. . . . The prohibition of certain things simply in virtue of their description as such-and-such identifiable kinds of action, regardless of any further consequences, is certainly not the whole of the Hebrew–Christian ethic; but is a noteworthy feature of it' (Anscombe 1968*a*: 197–8). See also Sidgwick 1907: 200. And one can, like W. D. Ross, hold that certain kinds of acts are always wrong (e.g. lying, breaking promises), while allowing that consequences can also have weight; see Ross 1930: 16–22; also Ross 1939: 134.

9. See Anscombe 1968*a*: 198.

10. See Anscombe 1968*b*: 287.

11. Thomas Nagel defends this sort of deontology in his 1986: ch. IX, sect. 5.

12. See Kagan 1989: 176: 'That is why the argument from respect must fail: it tries to claim that a certain kind of act's being disrespectful is the basis of its being unjustified. But I believe that the reverse is closer to the truth.'

13. This is Judith Jarvis Thomson's approach; see her 1990: ch. VII.

14. By a 'substantive theory' I mean one that would supply the existence conditions for a right. On the need for such a theory, see Griffin

1984. A substantive theory is what Judith Thomson needs for her argument in Thomson 1990, which, it seems to me, in the end she does not supply. In this connection, see Carl Wellman's (1992) review of her book.

15. I say more about this link in Ch. VIII, sect. 1.

16. Nagel 1980: 131–3.

17. For this characterization of virtue ethics, see Slote 1992: xiv, xix, 89; Hursthouse 1987: 220.

18. See MacIntyre 1992: 1277.

19. This idea has been developed independently, and quite differently, in Honoré 1993.

20. Important modern discussions of these issues are Bennett 1981; Bennett 1995; and Kagan 1989: esp. chs. 3 and 4.

CHAPTER VIII

1. See Ch. I, sect. 4.

2. Ibid.

3. I do not deny the complexity of what it is to 'describe' such a subject. There is a large element of interpretation in any description. There are complications in moving from one level of description to another, at which new entities and processes may appear, the relations of which to old entities and processes can be difficult to plot (I discuss this a bit in Ch. III). There are also doubts about various proposals of the 'unity' of the sciences. Still, despite all this, there is extensive functional unity.

4. See Ch. I, sect. 4.

5. See Ch. IV, sect. 2.

6. See Ch. V, sect. 3.

7. See Ch. IV, sect. 4.

8. This link was once the subject of much dispute. See, e.g. the two collections of articles Castañeda and Nakhnikian 1965 (esp. the papers by W. K. Frankena and W. D. Falk) and Wallace and Walker 1970 (esp. the paper by W. K. Frankena). See also the influential discussion in Hare 1963: ch. 8, sect. 4, esp. pp. 146–7.

9. However, one striking way in which the current use of the word 'moral' differs from some past uses is that it has become narrower. Morality, on our current conception, does not answer the general question, How should I live?, but the more specific one, How must I accommodate the interests of others? Not everyone likes the change (e.g. Williams 1985: ch. 1; see his distinction between 'ethics' (broader) and 'morality' (narrower) on pp. 6 ff.). It seems to be a uniquely

modern Western concern as to how we are to distinguish morality from prudence or aesthetics or etiquette. In classical Chinese or ancient Greek ethical writing it is hard to find sharp distinctions being drawn between moral views and other beliefs about how to live, or indeed any analogue to our current narrow conception of 'morality'. (On this, see Kupperman 1986: ch. 1, esp. p. 7.) Should we in the modern West regret this narrowing? I think not. It is true that, in separating morality sharply from any satisfactorily rich account of individual flourishing, one can grossly oversimplify moral deliberation. That separation has also served to deny morality access to, among other things, any realistic conception of human agency. These have been great losses. But to prevent them, we do not have to give up our current conception of morality. We have, instead, to be sure that we also have an adequate conception of prudence and of agency.

10. The Aristotelian, Christian, Marxist, and rights traditions have all been called upon. For a survey of writing about the environment from different ethical traditions, see Attfield and Dell 1989.

11. See Ch. V, sects. 3–5.

12. For a brief history of modernism's 'abstract individual' and opposition to it, see Taylor 1975: ch. 1. For a fuller history, see Taylor 1989: pts. II–V. Charles Taylor has his own strong arguments against the 'abstract individual' (called by him the 'disengaged identity' of modern naturalism) in e.g. the introduction to Taylor 1985: esp. p. 8.

13. I discuss hedonist and preference accounts of well-being (and other accounts in the same broadly utilitarian tradition) in Griffin 1986: chs. I and II.

14. See the discussion in Ch. II and also in Griffin 1991a.

BIBLIOGRAPHY

Anscombe, G. E. M. (1957), *Intention*, Oxford: Blackwell.

—— (1968*a*), 'Modern Moral Philosophy', in J. J. Thomson and G. Dworkin (eds.), *Ethics*, New York: Harper and Row.

—— (1968*b*), 'Two Kinds of Error in Action', in J. J. Thomson and G. Dworkin (eds.), *Ethics*, New York: Harper and Row.

Aristotle, *Nicomachean Ethics*.

Arrow, Kenneth J. (1984), 'Utility and Expectation in Economic Behaviour', in *Collected Papers of Kenneth J. Arrow*, vol. 3, Oxford: Blackwell.

Attfield, R. and K. Dell (1989) (eds.), *Values, Conflict, and the Environment*, Ian Ramsey Centre Publication no. 2, Oxford: Ian Ramsey Centre.

Baldwin, Thomas (1985), 'Ethical Non-Naturalism', in Ian Hacking (ed.), *Exercises in Analysis*, Cambridge: Cambridge University Press.

Bennett, Jonathan (1981), 'Morality and Consequences', in S. M. McMurrin (ed.), *The Tanner Lectures on Human Values (1981)*, Salt Lake City: University of Utah Press.

—— (1995), *The Act Itself*, Oxford: Clarendon Press.

Blackburn, Simon (1981), 'Reply: Rule-Following and Moral Reasoning', in S. Holtzman and C. Leich (eds.), *Wittgenstein: To Follow a Rule*, London: Routledge and Kegan Paul.

—— (1984), *Spreading the Word*, Oxford: Clarendon Press.

Blanshard, Brand (1939), *The Nature of Thought*, 2 vols., London: Allen and Unwin.

Bonjour, Laurence (1985), *The Structure of Empirical Knowledge*, Cambridge, Mass.: Harvard University Press.

Bradley, F. H. (1914), *Essays on Truth and Reality*, Oxford: Oxford University Press.

Brandt, R. B. (1979), *A Theory of the Good and the Right*, Oxford: Clarendon Press.

—— (1985), 'Criteria for Explications of Moral Language', in D. Copp and D. Zimmerman (eds.), *Morality, Reason and Truth*, Totowa, NJ: Rowman and Allanheld.

Brink, David (1989), *Moral Realism and the Foundations of Ethics*, Cambridge: Cambridge University Press.

Castañeda, H. N. and G. Nakhnikian (1965) (eds.), *Morality and the Language of Conduct*, Detroit: Wayne State University Press.

Charles, David and Kathleen Lennon (1992) (eds.), Introduction to *Reduction, Explanation, and Realism*, Oxford: Clarendon Press.

Dancy, Jonathan (1985), *Introduction to Contemporary Epistemology*, Oxford: Blackwell.

—— (1993), *Moral Reasons*, Oxford: Blackwell.

Daniels, Norman (1979), 'Wide Reflective Equilibrium and Theory Acceptance in Ethics', *Journal of Philosophy* 76.

Davidson, Donald (1980), *Essays on Actions and Events*, Oxford: Clarendon Press.

—— (1982), 'Expressing Evaluations', Lindley Lecture, Kansas: University of Kansas Press, 1982.

Dummett, Michael (1991), *The Logical Basis of Metaphysics*, London: Duckworth.

Flanagan, Owen (1991), *Varieties of Moral Personality*, Cambridge, Mass.: Harvard University Press.

Foot, Philippa (1978), *Virtues and Vices*, Oxford: Blackwell.

Freud, Sigmund (1957), *Civilization and Its Discontents*, London: Hogarth Press.

Gauthier, David (1963), *Practical Reasoning*, Oxford: Clarendon Press.

Gibbard, Allan (1990), *Wise Choices, Apt Feelings*, Oxford: Clarendon Press.

Giddens, Anthony (1977), *Studies in Social and Political Theory*, London: Hutchinson.

—— (1993), *New Rules of Sociological Method*, 2nd edn., Cambridge: Cambridge University Press.

Glover, Jonathan (1977), *Causing Death and Saving Lives*, Harmondsworth: Penguin.

Goldman, Alan H. (1988), *Moral Knowledge*, London: Routledge.

Gordon, R. M. (1987), *The Structure of Emotions*, Cambridge: Cambridge University Press.

Grice, H. P. (1991), *The Concept of Value*, Oxford: Clarendon Press.

Griffin, James (1984), 'Towards a Substantive Theory of Rights', in R. G. Frey (ed.), *Utility and Rights*, Minneapolis: University of Minnesota Press.

—— (1986), *Well-Being*, Oxford: Clarendon Press.

—— (1990), Review of Shelly Kagan, *The Limits of Morality*, *Mind* 99.

—— (1991*a*), 'Against the Taste Model', in J. Elster and J. Roemer (eds.), *Interpersonal Comparisons of Well-Being*, Cambridge: Cambridge University Press.

—— (1991*b*), 'Mixing Values', *Proceedings of the Aristotelian Society*, suppl. vol. 65.

—— (1992*a*), 'The Human Good and the Ambitions of Consequentialism', *Social Philosophy and Policy* 9.

—— (1992*b*), 'Values: Reduction, Supervenience, and Explanation by Ascent', in D. Charles and K. Lennon (eds.), *Reduction, Explanation, and Realism*, Oxford: Clarendon Press.

—— (forthcoming *a*), 'Incommensurability: What's the Problem?', in Ruth Chang (ed.), *Incommensurability and Value*, Cambridge, Mass.: Harvard University Press.

—— (forthcoming *b*), 'Méta-ethique et éthique substantielle', in Monique Canto-Sperber (ed.), *Dictionnaire de Philosophie Morale*, Paris: Presses Universitaires de France.

Haack, Susan (1993), *Evidence and Inquiry*, Oxford: Blackwell.

Hare, R. M. (1952), *The Language of Morals*, Oxford: Clarendon Press.

—— (1963), *Freedom and Reason*, Oxford: Clarendon Press.

—— (1971), *Essays on Philosophical Method*, London: Macmillan.

—— (1981), *Moral Thinking*, Oxford: Clarendon Press.

—— (1984*a*), 'Reply to J. L. Mackie', in R. G. Frey (ed.), *Utility and Rights*, Minneapolis: University of Minnesota Press.

—— (1984*b*), 'Supervenience', *Proceedings of the Aristotelian Society*, suppl. vol. 55.

Harman, Gilbert (1977), *The Nature of Morality*, New York: Oxford University Press.

—— (1985), 'Is There a Single True Morality?', in D. Copp and D. Zimmerman (eds.), *Morality, Reason and Truth*, Totowa, NJ: Rowman and Allanheld.

Hempel, Carl (1967), *Philosophy of Natural Science*, Englewood Cliffs, NJ: Prentice-Hall.

Herman, Barbara (1993), *The Practice of Moral Judgement*, Cambridge, Mass.: Harvard University Press.

Hintikka, Jaako (1967) (ed.), *The Philosophy of Mathematics*, Oxford: Oxford University Press.

Hofstadter, D. and D. Dennett (1982) (eds.), *The Mind's I*, Harmondsworth: Penguin Books.

Honoré, T. (1993), 'The Dependence of Morality on Law', *Oxford Journal of Legal Studies* 13.

Hume, David, *A Treatise on Human Nature*.

—— *Enquiries Concerning the Human Understanding and Concerning the Principles of Morals*.

Hurley, Susan (1989), *Natural Reasons*, New York: Oxford University Press.

Hursthouse, Rosalind (1987), *Beginning Lives*, Oxford: Blackwell.

Kagan, Shelly (1989), *The Limits of Morality*, Oxford: Clarendon Press.

Kant, Immanuel (1961), *Groundwork of the Metaphysic of Morals*, trans. H. J. Paton, published with commentary as *The Moral Law*, London: Hutchinson.

—— (1970), 'On the Common Saying: "This May Be True in Theory, but It Does not Apply in Practice"', in H. Reiss (ed.), *Kant's Political Writings*, Cambridge: Cambridge University Press.

Katz, J. J. (1964), 'Semantic Theory and the Meaning of "Good"', *Journal of Philosophy* 61.

Korsgaard, Christine (1993), 'The Reasons We Can Share: An Attack on the Distinction between Agent-Relative and Agent-Neutral Reasons', *Social Philosophy and Policy* 10.

Kupperman, Joel (1986), *The Foundations of Morality*, London: Allen and Unwin.

Lakatos, I. (1963–4), 'Proofs and Refutations', *British Journal for the Philosophy of Science* 14.

Layard, P. R. G. and A. A. Walters (1978), *Micro-Economic Theory*, New York: McGraw-Hill.

Lehrer, Keith (1990), *Theory of Knowledge*, London: Routledge.

Lu, Li (1990), *Moving the Mountain: My Life in China, from the Cultural Revolution to Tiananmen Square*, London: Macmillan.

MacIntyre, Alasdair (1992), 'Virtue Ethics', in L. C. Becker and C. B. Becker (eds.), *Encyclopedia of Ethics*, Chicago: St James Press.

Mackie, J. L. (1976), 'Sidgwick's Pessimism', *Philosophical Quarterly* 26.

—— (1977), *Ethics*, Harmondsworth: Penguin.

—— (1984), 'Rights, Utility and Universalization', in R. G. Frey (ed.), *Utility and Rights*, Minneapolis: University of Minnesota Press.

McDowell, John (1981), 'Non-Cognitivism and Rule-Following', in S. Holtzman and C. Leich (eds.), *Wittgenstein: To Follow a Rule*, London: Routledge and Kegan Paul.

—— (1985), 'Values and Secondary Qualities', in T. Honderich (ed.), *Morality and Objectivity*, London: Routledge and Kegan Paul.

McNaughton, D. and P. Rawlings (1991–2), 'Honoring and Promoting Values', *Ethics* 102.

Moore, G. E. (1903), *Principia Ethica*, Cambridge: Cambridge University Press.

—— (1942), 'Reply to My Critics', in P. A. Schilpp (ed.), *The Philosophy of G. E. Moore*, La Salle, Ill.: Open Court.

Murdoch, Iris (1970), *The Sovereignty of Good*, London: Routledge and Kegan Paul.

Nagel, Thomas (1970), *The Possibility of Altruism*, Oxford: Clarendon Press.

—— (1980), 'The Limits of Objectivity', in S. M. McMurrin (ed.), *The Tanner Lectures on Human Values 1980*, Salt Lake City: University of Utah Press.

—— (1986), *The View from Nowhere*, New York: Oxford University Press.

—— (1991), *Equality and Partiality*, New York: Oxford University Press.

Newton-Smith, W. (1981), *The Rationality of Science*, London: Routledge and Kegan Paul.

Niebuhr, Reinhold (1956), *An Interpretation of Christian Ethics*, New York: Meridian Books.

Nozick, Robert (1981), *Philosophical Explanations*, Oxford: Clarendon Press.

Oliner, S. and P. Oliner (1988), *The Altruistic Personality: Rescuers of Jews in Nazi Europe*, New York: Free Press.

O'Neill, Onora (1989), *Constructions of Reason*, Cambridge: Cambridge University Press.

Parfit, Derek (1984), *Reasons and Persons*, Oxford: Clarendon Press.

Pettit, Philip (1991), 'Consequentialism', in P. Singer (ed.), *A Companion to Ethics*, Oxford: Blackwell.

Quine, W. V. (1953), *From a Logical Point of View*, Cambridge, Mass.: Harvard University Press.

Railton, Peter (1986), 'Moral Realism', *Philosophical Review* 95.

—— (1989), 'Naturalism and Prescriptivity', *Social Philosophy and Policy* 7.

Rawls, John (1951), 'Outline for a Decision Procedure for Ethics', *Philosophical Review* 60.

—— (1972), *A Theory of Justice*, Oxford: Clarendon Press.

Rawls, John (1974–5), 'The Independence of Moral Theory', *Proceedings and Addresses of the American Philosophical Association* 48.

—— (1980), 'Kantian Constructivism in Moral Theory', *Journal of Philosophy* 77.

—— (1985), 'Justice as Fairness: Political not Metaphysical', *Philosophy and Public Affairs* 14.

Raz, Joseph (1986), *The Morality of Freedom*, Oxford: Clarendon Press.

Rorty, Richard (1980), *Philosophy and the Mirror of Nature*, Oxford: Blackwell.

Ross, W. D. (1930), *The Right and the Good*, Oxford: Clarendon Press.

—— (1939), *Foundations of Ethics*, Oxford: Clarendon Press.

Russell, Bertrand (1906–7), 'On the Nature of Truth', *Proceedings of the Aristotelian Society* 7.

Sandel, Michael (1982), *Liberalism and the Limits of Justice*, Cambridge: Cambridge University Press.

Scanlon, T. M. (1978), 'Rights, Goals, and Fairness', in S. Hampshire (ed.), *Public and Private Morality*, Cambridge: Cambridge University Press.

Sidgwick, Henry (1907), *The Methods of Ethics*, 7th edn., London: Macmillan.

Simpson, A. W. B. (1984), *Cannibalism and the Common Law*, Chicago: University of Chicago Press.

Singer, Peter (1974), 'Sidgwick and Reflective Equilibrium', *Monist* 58.

Slote, Michael (1992), *From Morality to Virtue*, New York: Oxford University Press.

Smart, J. J. C. and Bernard Williams (1973), *Utilitarianism: For and Against*, Cambridge: Cambridge University Press.

Snare, Francis (1992), *The Nature of Moral Thinking*, London: Routledge.

Sprigge, T. L. S. (1988), *The Rational Foundation of Ethics*, London: Routledge and Kegan Paul.

Stampe, Dennis (1987), 'The Authority of Desire', *Philosophical Review* 96.

Sumner, L. W. (1992), 'Welfare, Happiness, and Pleasure', *Utilitas* 4.

Taylor, Charles (1975), *Hegel*, Cambridge: Cambridge University Press.

—— (1985), *Philosophical Papers*, vol. 1, Cambridge: Cambridge University Press.

—— (1989), *Sources of the Self*, Cambridge: Cambridge University Press.

Thomson, Judith Jarvis (1975–6), 'Killing, Letting Die, and the Trolley Problem', *Monist* 59.

—— (1990), *The Realm of Rights*, Cambridge, Mass.: Harvard University Press.

Updike, John (1990), *Self-Consciousness*, Harmondsworth: Penguin.

Wallace, G. and A. D. M. Walker (1970) (eds.), *The Definition of Morality*, London: Methuen.

Warnock, G. J. (1971), *The Object of Morality*, London: Methuen.

Wellman, Carl (1992), Review of Judith Jarvis Thomson, *The Realm of Rights*, *Journal of Philosophy* 89.

Westermarck, E. (1932), *Ethical Relativity*, London: Kegan Paul, Trench, Trubner.

Wiggins, David (1987), *Needs, Values, Truth*, Oxford: Blackwell.

—— (1990–1), 'Moral Cognitivism, Moral Relativism and Motivating Moral Beliefs', *Proceedings of the Aristotelian Society* 91.

Williams, Bernard (1981), *Moral Luck*, Cambridge: Cambridge University Press.

—— (1985), *Ethics and the Limits of Philosophy*, London: Fontana.

Wittgenstein, Ludwig (1953), *Philosophical Investigations*, trans. G. E. M. Anscombe, Oxford: Blackwell.

—— (1967), *Zettel*, trans. G. E. M. Anscombe, Oxford: Blackwell.

—— (1969), *On Certainty*, trans. Denis Paul and G. E. M. Anscombe, Oxford: Blackwell.

Wollheim, Richard (1984), *The Thread of Life*, Cambridge: Cambridge University Press.

Wright, Crispin (1988), 'Moral Values, Projection and Secondary Qualities', *Proceedings of the Aristotelian Society*, suppl. vol. 62.

—— (1992), *Truth and Objectivity*, Cambridge, Mass.: Harvard University Press.

Ziff, Paul (1960), *Semantic Analysis*, Ithaca, NY: Cornell University Press.

INDEX